For
Rhyme
&
Reason

A Poetic Journey of Life, Love, & Loss

by
Brian W. Woodward

Published by Hemingway Publisher
Printed in United States of America

Dedication

This collection is dedicated to my wife Shannon who is my inspiration and my heart. Without whom I would not have the intestinal fortitude to continue on as I do. I Love You!!!

Nancy M. Brown and Deborah Ann Wampler Burchel for their encouragement and continued support, and my loving mother Mrs. Myrtle L. Woodward who always believed in me...

Cover Art by Tyler B. Woodward.

Biography

Brian W. Woodward is a Christian American author and United States Air Force Veteran, celebrated for his diverse talents as a cabinet builder, kitchen & bath designer, and aspiring writer. At 60, he cherishes over 30 years of marriage, sharing the joy of four grown children. Brian's passions range from baseball and freshwater fishing to woodworking and writing, all intertwined with a deep love for the outdoors and his cherished dogs and cats. With literary inspirations like Edgar Allan Poe and Emily Dickinson, he revels in historical fiction, Western tales, and poetry. This anthology marks his earnest pursuit of a lifelong dream to become an author, combining his diverse experiences and passions into a compelling narrative.

Table of Contents

"A Brand New Day"

July 18th, 2023

A brand new day is dawning
And I'm thankful for the Sun
After a long night of storming
My new life has begun

Every day is a Blessing
And for this I am grateful
For the coffee in my cup
And the food on my table

As I look out of my window
I'm enjoying the view
Thinking of the list of things
I know I have to do

But first I give thanks
To the Lord above
For all His many Blessings
And the Gift of His Love

Things that I cannot repay
With my human hands
But I know that today
For Him, I take a stand

And as I watch the morning dew
Get dried up by the sun
I think of how for me and you
God gave his only Son

To save us from our sins
And give us an eternal home
And so that we may know
That we are never alone

So, get down on your knees
And bow your head in prayer
Be thankful he has met your needs
And that he is always there

So, get up and get going
As a brand new day awaits
And be happy in the knowing
At the end are Heaven's Gates

"Amen"

"A Buck or Two"

August 1st, 2023

Remember when we were young
And all the things we'd do
Just to keep ourselves busy
And make a buck or two

I recall that in the summers
Collecting beer and soda bottles
From back behind the bars
Boy! The smell was awful!

Sitting around the feed store
Loading the trucks and cars
For a bag of chips, and a soda
And maybe a candy bar

Going from house to house
With the mower and a can of gas
Raking leaves and pine straw
Pulling weeds and cutting grass

Aluminum cans and copper wire
Clearing brush and cutting wood
Picking and loading watermelons
Just anything that we could

We always had a few dollars
And we always knew
Just what all it took
To earn a buck or two...

"A Few Short Years"

July 23rd, 2023

Just a few short years ago
On a night just like tonight
I sat and thought and wondered
What heaven must be like

It couldn't be as hot
As it is right here
And if it was it would be hell
But, that's not what I hear

So, I closed my eyes and envisioned
The most beautiful of places
With a sky so clear and blue
And with wide open spaces

And water so cold and sweet
That I could almost taste it
With blue-green grass beneath my feet
What a wonderful oasis

With birds singing in the trees
The most beautiful of songs
And a choir of angels in harmony
I wanted to sing along

All of God's creatures
Just wandering about
The most marvelous of features
A miracle no doubt

And every little child
That had died when they were young
Was running free and wild
A brand new body won

With no signs of illnesses
Decease or of pain
The epitome of wellness
No discomfort or disdain

And all the older people
With bodies weak and worn
Were given brand new lives
Like babies newly born

And every pet that was ever loved
Came running so excited
To their master's open arms
Happy and delighted

So hear me now when I shout
A joyous place of bliss
Lies just beyond the fear and doubt
A Heaven does exist

So, if you want to go there
Here's what you have to do
Take Jesus as your Savior
And to him be true

There's room enough for everyone
That calls upon his name
Rich or poor, old or young
He loves you just the same

So ask me if there's a place to go
When this life is o'er
And I'll say, "If you follow Jesus
You'll walk through Heaven's door"...

"A Garden Full of Roses"

August 1st, 2023

If I had a rose for every person
That I have ever loved
Who has passed from this world
To Heaven up above

I'd have a garden full of roses
Of every shape and size
Every color represented
Right before my eyes

Most of my old friends
And close family have gone
On to be with Jesus
For eternity to live on

Now I am still here
Living one day at a time
With my garden full of roses
And my memories so sublime

I know someday soon
I too will become a rose
In someone else's garden
And live in their memories I suppose...

4

"A Knight to Remember"

August 13th, 2023

I am a knight to remember
Lest you dare forget
Never a pawn to play
In life's game of chess

I serve but one king and queen
Them alone will I protect
Often sacrificing myself
But what else would you expect

Many moves are to be made
In this game of life
And many lives to save
Some with more love than strife

If you see me on the battlefield
To not try to fight me or engage
My wrath is swift and furious
And my anger you will enrage

If in the end there is but one left
To be called before the throne
And that one is me I say
To stand there all alone

A man should be loved strong and deep
So, kiss me now before I into battle go
To fight my mortal enemies
With no mercy to them I show

Will I live or will I die
I do not know my fate
Yet I will ride on gallantly
For I was never one to wait

Attack, always attack
From their right or from their left
Catching them off guard
Never letting them get set

Alas, the king is in danger
He is left undefended
Here I come my liege
The game has not ended

Into the storm do I ride
On my steed so white
My armor glistening in the sun
I blind them with my light

The battle is soon over
And my king still stands
Although his queen is lost
I hope he will understand

My job is now over
And so I do retire
To my quarters will I go
And my love that I desire

I am met with a warm embrace
And a kiss oh so tender
I am the one, do not forget
I am a Knight to Remember!!!

"A Little Nuts"

July 26th, 2023

Every single day
I watch this same squirrel
Just one of God's creatures
With whom I share this world

Now this little fellow
Is very persistent
He never quits trying
Even though I am insistent

About the fact
That I do not want him to
Get into my bird feeder
And eat up all their food

On several occasions
He's come so very close
And I just sit and watch
With my thumb to my nose

Now I guess where I am going
With this little spat
Is that there's a lesson here
About just where I'm at

I keep trying and trying
But to no avail
To get something accomplished
And move on up the trail

I guess the point
That I am trying to make
Is that I have to change things up
Or I'll make the same mistake

The Lord put that squirrel
Directly in my path
To show me that I'm a little nuts
To keep trying that

Now I have since changed my ways
And my point of view
And I encourage you
To do the same thing too

If you always do
The same thing every time
And you never get anywhere
You just might find

That you're a little nuts
And just a little blind
To the facts about what you
Are doing wrong all the time

This world is a great teacher
And she's as tough as they come
You'll always be in school
And that's the reason to become

Nobody's fool
Including your own
And you too can be a winner
On a stage all alone

We all start out a little nuts
With great visions of grandeur
But then we grow into a tree
Full of grace and splendor

So do not be afraid
To grow out of your shell
Because you'll find that when you do
You're going to be just swell...

"A Loved Ones Pain"

July 4th, 2023

What do you say in times like these
When a loved one is in pain
We just get down on our knees
And pray this prayer again;

Dear Heavenly Father, thank you
For all the blessings that you give
And for our Salvation
And the lives that we live

And Lord, all the pain and suffering
We know that you endured
To save us from eternal pain
Of this we rest assured

Although we are not sure
All of the reasons why
Pain and suffering must go on
While You Reign on High

We place into your Mighty Hands
The things we can't control
And pray for yet another day
Your Healing to unfold

We pray for Peace and Understanding
When times like these prevail
And consume those we treasure
And our faith begins to fail

And strength to hold them in our Hearts
When their time is drawing near
And ask, Oh! Lord thy will be done
For those we hold so dear

So, Father, hold them to your heart
As you alone know their fate
Then bind them not unto this Earth
But, through Your Heaven's Gates

Amen! And again I say Amen!

"A Mother's Daily Struggle"

December 6th, 2019

Her day begins and ends
With a simple prayer
Knowing that at least
Her God will be there

The last one to bed
And the first one to rise
A sleepwalking Saint
In her children's eyes

A never-ending struggle
To keep it all together
With food on the table
In all kinds of weather

Despite all the obstacles
That gets in her way
She manages to make it
Through one more day

She smiles when she's hurting
Just to cover her pain
Gives thanks to the Lord
When he brings the rain

To water her garden
That she tends with care
And a bucket of water
To wash her hair

From the earliest of dawns
Until the latest of nights
She works constantly
To keep on the lights

With the children all fed
And clothes on the line
She can't stop to rest
For there isn't the time

With dishes all done
And the children in bed
With a moment alone
She bows her head

Asking the Lord
For all she must do
A little more strength
Just to make it through

Trusting in Him
And seeking his face
And thanking Him for
His saving grace, Amen...

"A Nannies Love"

July 7th, 2023

A Nannies Love is forever true
And it holds you oh so close
And scolds the bad things you do
With just a tweak on your nose
The baking smells of cookies and pies
That lingers on her clothes and in her house
And that sparkle that she gets in her eyes
When her grandchildren are all about
Memories that last through the years
That never seems to fade
Why it seems like only yesterday
That with you she played
Checkers and dominoes
Which she rarely lets you win
That competitive spirit that made you
Into women and into men
So hold on to those memories
Because when you are gray and old
They'll keep you reminiscing
And give you something on which to hold...

"A New Friend"

July 21st, 2023

Have you ever been alone
Somewhere on the street
When out of the blue clear sky
A new friend you meet

Someone whom you've never known
In this lifetime or the past
But, somehow form a bond
That for a lifetime lasts

Kindred spirits maybe
But, who really knows
How these things happen
Or just where things will go

Jesus was the kind of man
Whom others thronged to see
But it was all in God's plan
For He and I to meet

I've known Him for a lifetime
From a very young age
And I knew right when I met him
That He my life had saved

For a very special purpose
That I still do not quite know
But my life is in His service
And His Love I try to show

So, if you are lonesome
And need a lifelong friend
Jesus is the answer
He'll be with you till the end

And if you are faithful
In his following
A heavenly home awaits you
With much rejoicing

So, be not downtrodden
As you walk along your way
If you need a friend
He is there to stay

So, look all around you
Wherever you may be
And if you look hard enough
A New Friend you'll surely meet!!!

"A Single Act of Kindness"

22 March 2017

Today I met a man
Who seemed to have less than I
And after a warm meal
I was soon to realize

That he was no worse for wear
And he was not forlorn
He seemed to be in good spirits
Although his clothes were old and worn

His shoes were down at heel
But, when the opportunity came
He prayed before his meal
And I did the same

I could have tried to judge him
But, it is just not my place
When I know that one day
God will judge me to my face

So, I helped a kind old beggar
Get through a long hard day
And with a smile and a handshake
He went along his way

For all I know this was God
And he came back here to see
If I had learned anything at all
From the life He'd given me

It doesn't really take much
To change someone's life
A simple smile or subtle touch
In the midst of their strife

So be all you can be
Each and every day
Let God's love shine through you
As you travel along your way...

"A Single Rose"

August 13th, 2023

I am but a single rose
In the garden of your love
And after many seasons
You chose me from thereof
She loves me

You cut me tenderly from the vine
Separated me from the rest
And despite my prickly thorns
Held me close to your chest
She loves me not

You took me home and gently
Groomed me up and down my stem
And then put me in a pretty vase
With some water therein
She loves me

You watched bloom gradually
From a bud to a blossom
And the fragrance I emitted
Was nothing less than awesome
She loves me not

That was for but a season
And I slowly began to fade
Then you kindly removed me
From my beautiful vase
She loves me

You took my fallen petals
Then you put them in a quiet place
And you stored me for a while
Where I could not see your face
She loves me not

The kind and tender way
That you handled my demise
Meant so much to me
That my love just wouldn't die
She loves me

Now, in my quiet place
My aroma just got stronger
And when you opened up my box
I could not contain it any longer
She loves me not

You took my dried-out pedals
Into your magic hands
And you pressed them in a cloth
And I began to understand
She loves me

The love you gave to me
Made me live on after death
And now my fragrance lingers
You smell with every inward breath
She loves me not

So, now my love burns like incense
In this light and lovely space
I live on in your memories
And in the smile on your face
She loves me!!!

"A Stormy Night"

July 17th, 2023

On a stormy night when no stars are out
And the thunder and lightning dance about
The rain comes down in blinding sheets
Where mother Earth and Heavens meet
The big drops land and splash around
Making puddles on the ground
The wind tosses to and fro
The trees and shrubs far below
From valley low to mountain grand
Mother Nature cleanses the whole land
Till she plays out and hurries past
Leaving peace on the earth at last
As dawn arrives and the sun peeks
Its sleepy head from the cloudy sheets
A brand new day crisp and clean
A sky so blue and grass so green
The flowers bloom as if to say
Hello to those who come their way

So curse not the raging storm
For in its wake you'll find
A peaceful feeling that is born
To benefit all mankind

"A Stranger"

July 27th, 2023

The other morning I saw a stranger
And as I passed him in the neighborhood
I did not recognize him
But I thought that I should

His hair was all which-a-away
And his beard was kind of rough
His eyes were tired and glassy
And seemed kind of gruff

I've heard stories about him
From people here and there
And the tales that I got from them
Were that we should all beware

This fellow it seems
Was not the type at all
To say something nice
If you met him at the mall

He was extremely impolite
And was considered very greedy
And he was just as rude
When approached by the needy

A modern day Scrooge
That we should all avoid
Especially around the holidays
A regular bundle of joy

Very cold and clammy
Were his boney hands
And his cothes were torn and tattered
Even though he was a moneyed man

Just what kind of person
Can even live this way
Or go about his business
In such a calloused way

So I thought I'd get to know him
And take a little time
Spend a penny for his thoughts
They ended up costing me a dime

He wasn't much different than I was
Not too many years ago
When he just quit caring
About people don't you know

He said they were too clingy
So he pushed them all away
And now he is all alone
He likes it better this way

Then I introduced him to my Savior
And his eyes got big and bright
He seemed to be melting
Way down deep inside

His old cold heart got lighter
Deep inside his chest
And then he showed me a picture
In a watch from his vest

He said that he had once been married
And he told me her name
It was Faith and she was quite beautiful
But she was gone and it wouldn't be the same

They say he is a hoarder
Of silver and of gold
And he never gives
To those who are poor and old

She just couldn't tolerate
His wicked evil ways
Saving all his money
For a rainy day

They had once been very happy
In their big house down by the lake
And they had huge flower garden
With big walls and wrought iron gates

He built for her a prison
And he tried to keep her in
Protecting her from the world
Her family and her friends

But one day she was gone
Like a feather on the breeze
Now he was all alone
With just his memories

He had nothing left to live for
His heart grew heavy and cold
And as pushed everyone away
He began to grow cynical and old

And he never went back to the garden
When the flowers began to bloom
He just counted all his money
In the corner of his room

So, I told him my story
About my salvation and my God
And how my life that was much like his
Had changed me for the good

He listened very intently
And I have to give him this
He did not interrupt me
While I told him of my bliss

So, that day then and there
He turned his life around
And he gave away all his money
To a local charity he'd found

His attitude towards people changed
And now he lends a helping hand
To all of those in need

Any time that he can

I don't think you'd know him
If you passed him on the street
He has a sparkle in his eyes
And he's eager to greet

People that used to avoid him
Now flock to his door
To view his flower garden
As they never had before

And then one day I saw him
With a fair lady on his arm
And she was just as beautiful
As the day she had fallen for his charms

All those years ago
When they were young in life
And then when he saw me
He quickly introduced his wife

She was Oh! So delighted
As she shook my hand
And when they walked on down the street
He turned and smiled again

You see Jesus has that effect on folks
Who are cold at heart
He reaches down and touches them
And saves them where they are!!!

"After Dark"

August 11th, 2013

After dark when the lights go out
I get out of bed and creep about
From place to place in shadows deep
While everyone else is fast asleep

A starry night with a sky so clear
A harvest moon that seems so near
The fog drifts in and settles down
The dew falls softly to the ground

Crickets chirp and cicadas sing
The night's alive with everything
A spider weaves her web so tight
The hapless fly gives up the fight

A mother doe and spotted fawn step into the glade
To eat their fill before the dawn and the darkness fades
A pair of bunnies bounce around in the grass so wet
The sly old fox waits his chance he'll have his dinner yet

Barefoot I feel between my toes the mud from by the creek
I slip and trip and nearly fall and almost start to speak
Then silently I wander cross field and meadow grand
To hilltop yon I make my way and there I make my stand

Sometimes I see the shooting stars
They come so close and yet so far
I stare up at the heavens and can't but wonder how
God made it all in just six days!!! Well what's he doing now?

"All Day I Sit and Dream"

December 3rd, 2013

All day I sit and dream
Of wonderful far off shores
Where there is no longer fighting
And men have laid down their swords

Where women sing in the sunshine
As they carry on throughout the day
And children run through the hedges
And sing and shout as they play

Of awesome towering peaks
Laden with luscious grasses of green
And sights so magically marvelous
You just can't believe what you've seen

Where the wind is so crisp and sweet
That you can't wash it down in a breath
Where the kiss of butterfly is such a treat
And you haven't seen anything yet

And the songs of the angels in motion
That you long to hear some more
The waves so blue on the ocean
And sand so white on the shore

The forests so lush and valleys so deep
And mountains so broad and wide
The creatures are all so gentle and sweet
That they all just seem to abide

Where the streets are all paved with pure gold
And the rivers all run with pure light
This is the place that I want to go
When I am through with this life

So, where is this place that I dream of
That I think of both night and day
Where there's room enough for all of us
Why, it's just a breath away

So, just how do you get there
What road must you take
Up this path that's rocky and rough
You will surely find the way

And if you pass this way you will see
That it's all right here waiting,
Waiting for you and for me
So, I sit here anticipating

So if you give your heart to Him
Then I know that you'll find
Eternal Life, through Jesus Christ
In the Holy City of Zion

"All of God's Creations"

July 25th, 2023

All of God's Creations
Creatures great and small
Deserve a chance at life
God loves them one and all

From the tiniest of insects
To the largest of the herd
They each have a special purpose
God says this in his Word

Every microorganism
That has ever lived
Has had a reason to be here
And so much to give

From the plankton to the cosmos
He created it with care
To fulfill a mission
And our universe to share

So before you go on a rampage
To kill and destroy
Think about its purpose here
And the life that it enjoys

For we are not creators
Just the caretakers thereof
Of this planet that we live on
And the life that we love

For we all have a gift
And a responsibility
Leave it better than we found it
For all eternity

It seems so easy to just use it up
But what happens when it's gone
With nothing left for our children
But the words of a sad old song

Be careful of where you go
Even more so what you say
For words are like a two edge sword
Indiscriminate in what they slay

So I leave you folks
With this thought on your minds
Take nothing but the pictures
Leave only the memories behind

Have a blessed and joyous day
And be thankful for what you are
Because you are part of a bigger plan
As seen from a distant star

Thank you all for reading
This little ditty to the end
A lasting impression I hope
On all of you my Friends...

"Alone"
August 7th, 2023

People around
Talking loud
I am a ghost
In this crowd

Never speaking
Only hearing
Silently creeping
Disappearing

I feel dead
Far from gone
Crowded room
All alone...

"An Acorn"

July 30th, 2023

Right now it's just an acorn
Hanging in an old oak tree
Surround up there by
Branches, twigs and leaves

But soon it will be ready
To fall to the earth
And fulfill its destiny
In the fertile dirt

Seasons come and go
And as time passes by
The rains bring the water
When the land is dry

The acorn was just a seed
When it started on this quest
But then sprouts into a seedling
And now it starts the test

It must struggle from now on
For nourishment and light
If it's to continue to grow
Up to its potential height

Fast forward one hundred years
Now it's tall and strong
And taken its rightful place
In the forest where it belongs

We are all just an acorn
When we are brought into this world
To grow into a mighty oak
Our limbs and leaves to unfurl

And just like the mighty oak
In the forest grand
We too must reach out to the Son
When we take our stand

We all have a purpose
And have fruit to bear
Some more than others
On this planet that we share...

"An Old Lady in a New World"

July 29th, 2923

I'm just an old lady in a new world
A lot to expect from a simple farm girl
Everything's moving at such a fast pace
It's like everyone is looking
For a sponsor in a car race

Way back in the day
Things were a lot less trouble
Wake up and go to work
Then work a double
If you wanted to eat then you'd never shirk

You just cannot do for yourself anymore
Everything that runs is computerized
That even includes vacuuming the floor
Nowadays things are so specialized
Let me introduce you to my RoboVac

From the time I get going
Till I fall back into bed
Someone is trying to get me setup
With all of latest technological gadgets
Makes me just want to throw up

Now it's so hard to get around
With all the new highways and byways
I cannot even get to the store
To do my all of my shopping
It doesn't make sense anymore

Something that is as simple
As washing your clothes
You must have a degree
Or you might just be thumbing your nose
At the whole automated industry

I used to work in an office
And letters and billing I would type
But nowadays those things are generated
By computers and the like
Secretarial knowledge has been upgraded

Even my TV and record player
Has a remote control
With so many buttons and choices
You never know which one to press and hold
Or heck! You can just use your voice

And even my new sewing machine
It has a little computer inside
It can sew things a mile a minute
I hardly understand
How to put the bobbin in it

Things today are so modernized
That I just want to spit
This new world is one big pain
And I'm about ready to split
I'm afraid of going insane

So you all can keep
Your new world
And I'll just hang on to mine
It's just too complicated for this old girl
I like my old world just fine!!!

"Andi's Song"

July 25th, 2023

Lord, I don't want to die
But if I'm Heaven bound
Grant me this one last wish
Before they lay me in the ground

Promise to take care
Of the ones I leave behind
Help them deal with the pain
That will haunt them time to time

I know that I am going
To a better place
On a beautiful new journey
Through time and space

Now that my life is over
And I'm free from all the strife
And I get a brand new body
In my glorious new life

In my lofty perch beside you
Up there on your throne
Let me keep watch over
Those I call my own

And Lord I do know
That it's all written in your plan
But there are some things
That we mortals don't understand

I thank for you the life that I've had
And the blessings that you've granted
Now Lord I trust that you
Will tend the seeds I've planted

And help them to mature and grow
In Peace and Love and Grace
And protect them Lord until the day
They too will see your face

Lord there are so many things
That I wanted to do
Like watch my children grow
And have children too

To know my first grandchild
To hold them in my arms
And to spoil them rotten
With all my special charms

Lord help them to know
That I am always near
Deep within their hearts
Let their memories stand clear

I know it's time for me to go
And be with you on High
But give me just one moment
To say all my goodbyes

Mom and Dad
I love you both so much
And I know that you'll be sad
But I will be in touch

With you both from time to time
When you're feeling blue
I'll fly down and lift you up
And I'll comfort you

And to all of my children
You know you are my heart
I've loved you from your conception
And I won't be too far

So, I have to go now
And take my rightful place
Beside the King of Kings
In my final resting place...

"Angels Without Your Wings"

August 3rd, 2023

Today I knocked
On Heaven's Door
For God to let me in
Over on the Golden Shore

But God said to me;
"It's not your time my friend
I need for you to go back
And finish what you began."

I said; "But Lord,
I'm already here and yet
I've waited so very long
And I have no regrets."

"Child, you have not finished
Your mission that I gave
And there are many others
Whose lives you need to save."

"I need your talents and your skills
To spread more of my Grace
To all of those who without you
Would never see my face"

I cried; "I can see the streets of Heaven
Made of gold right over there
Haven't I been a faithful servant?
I don't think that this is fair."

"My precious little child I know
You do not comprehend
That the journey that I sent you on
Has not yet come to its end"

So, here I sit in the seat
Of my smoldering ambulance
And I can see that I am injured
With just one quick glance

You see I'm a paramedic
And many lives depend on me
But it's just not my time to go
I've so more to do and be

Even though I am hurting
Broken up inside
I get out and go to check
On the person with whom I did collide

There's a family of three
The parents are both okay
A father, mother, and a child
But the baby is beginning to fade

I take him from the car
And then I resuscitate
Using all my tools and skills
He's alive for goodness sake

Then I walk up to Heaven's Door
Then my God says to me;
"Welcome Home my child
Your mission is now complete."

So, now I am walking down the streets of gold
Many people do I see
Whose lives had been extended
All because of me!!!

God Bless all our First Responders!!!
Angels without your Wings...

"Another Day"

July 23rd, 2023

Another day has come and gone
And your voice I did not hear
I don't know how to carry on
Without you being near

We spent so many years together
Like I always knew we would
The storms of life we weathered
And now you're gone for good

I know death's just an open door
That we all must pass through
A portal to that golden shore
That I want to walk with you

So when my time here on earth is o'er
Be waiting there for me
And we will stroll for ever more
In blissful harmony

To leave this world behind
I am not in a hurry
I'll be along in my good time
So you don't have to worry

There are many songs left unsung
And so much I have to give
So little time to get it done
And so much life to live

So many of life lessons
I have yet to teach
So many little sessions
So many souls left to reach

I'm trying hard to pace myself
For that final mile
And when the race is finally over
I can say with a smile

I did my best and I am proud
Of what I leave behind
As I look out over the crowd
Of family that is mine

And when I'm gone they all can say
"That when he went home to Glory
He left this world a better place"
What a beautiful life story

So wait for me I'll be along
And when I get to Heaven's door
I'll be whistling a song
And I'll be home forevermore...

"Butterflies & Flowers"

August 6th, 2023

Butterflies and Flowers
Are special gifts from God
To remind us to spread his love
Thanking Him for everything we've got

As the butterfly flutters from
Flower to flower it can spread
Life replenishing pollen that
Lingers long after each is dead

It's their lifelong ambition
And it should be ours
To spread God's love to everyone
Because even the weeds have flowers

We all have some beauty within us
Waiting for the right time to flourish
And when we His love and joy
We can also be nourished

Nothing stands to be lost
It's part of God's Master Plan
Even when we are being tossed
Do the best you can

For Life's wind and weather
Can easily carry us away
To people and places we didn't care
To visit on any given day

The point is this;

No matter where you find yourselves
Spread God's Love and Joy
It benefits everyone and everything
Man, woman, girl, and boy

For we are all butterflies and flowers
And we all have a purpose and a mission
And when we do our jobs right
It's a win-win situation

"Country Road"

July 30th, 2023

Have you slowly driven
Down a country road
Just to see where
It might happen to go

Let me tell you neighbor
It is a pure delight
Passing all the scenery
And seeing all the sights

Look there's a pasture
Full of dairy cows
Now we're behind
A tractor with a plow

A red barn with a star
Over the swinging doors
With a loft full of hay
And an old dirt floor

Check out all the chickens
Roaming far and wide
And all the baby goats
In the pen on the side

Now look at the hay fields
As far as the eye can see
And the way the shafts bend
In the summer breeze

Here's a field full of corn
And on for miles it goes
There's one of cotton
Just look at all the rows

Can you see the farmhouse
Back up there on the hill
With the white picket fence
Oh! What a thrill

It looks just like a postcard
That you might have seen
Or a Norman Rockwell painting
With the quiet little stream

Maybe stop and visit
And sit for just a spell
At one of the roadside stands
Where there's produce for sale

Have a cup of coffee
Lemonade or sweet iced tea
There's so much you can do
And so much you can see

So, take your time
As you go traveling
Because when you do
You won't miss a thing

Just remember this
When and where you go
There's always so much to see
Down a country road

...

"Daffodils & Dandelions"

August 19th, 2023

Daffodils & Dandelions
Not too much different you see
One is a beautiful flower
The other is a beautiful weed

The Daffodil is the one of the first
That typically blooms in the spring
And when they do, Oh! What a view
It's a very beautiful thing

The Dandelion however
Usually blooms in the fall
A very useful plant indeed
Why! You can eat it all

They are far distant cousins
And are very unique you see
The city and the country flowers
How much further apart could you be

The Daffodil is quite lovely
Usually the first flower of spring
Where Narcissus gets his name
Very self-indulging, but a very exquisite thing

Then there's the Dandelion
The workhorse of the breed
On one stem grows its flower
On the other grows its seed

The Dandelion is not indigenous
But a newcomer from overseas
Planted here by the pilgrims
Loved here by the bees

The whole plant is edible
From its flower to its roots
A great source of vitamins
And the last that blooms to boot

The Daffodil brings good fortune
And it symbolizes the coming of Easter
It means "A New Beginning"
And the rising of our Savior

All in all, they bring their beauty
For all the world to see
Together they bloom all year
Glorious in the first degree

So, now when you see a field of flowers
You'll know what's behind the scenes
Think about all of their beauty
And all of the joy that they bring

Thank you, Lord, for this gift of beauty
To remind us one and all
It's the little things that matter the most
Winter, spring, summer, and fall...

"Dear God"

July 24th, 2023

You pick me up, when I let you down
You lift me high into the sky
You let me see all around
The bigger picture of where and why

So many times I have left
Yet you always take me back
Deep into the cleft
You give me what I lack

You lead me and you guide me
Down life's narrow trail
You feed me and you hide me
From the evil that prevails

What values have I to thee?
My great and mighty king
I am the dust beneath your feet
You are the wind beneath my wings

But I thank you Lord for what I have
My home and family
The salvation from my past
All praise I give to thee...

"Desperately Seeking Me"

August 6th, 2023

I have been searching for myself
For so very, very long
But I am nowhere to be found
Since my heart has gone

You see it has been missing
For quite some time
And if it can't be found
I'm afraid I will lose my mind

It often seems to wander
From place to place
Searching for myself
In every stranger's face

But I can't seem to find me
No matter where I look
Nor is there a reflection
In the water of the brook

So, what does this mean
Am I just a ghost
A fleeting memory in the minds
Of the ones I love the most

Am I dead and gone
Or just in between lives
The one I lived before this
And the one I've yet to find

Where are all the answers to
These questions I possess
Is this a life exam
And will I pass the test

I just do not know
And I'm so perplexed
Where do I go
And what do I do next

In every nook and cranny
And I have journeyed far and wide
Looking for all the pieces
Of my shattered life

Just when I think I've found me
Something seems to occur
To scatter me all over to the
Four corners of the earth

So, now I'm floating aimlessly
From hither to yon
Desperately seeking me
Through eternity and beyond...

"Dreams"

June 2nd, 2013

When you drift off to sleep and your mind begins to roam
Across cloudy glen, and dale, to a place all your own
Here in your kingdom, as far as the eye can see
You are in your magic world, and can be anything you want to be
A knight in shining armor, to champion a cause
A conqueror of continents, that wins the applause
A pilot of a jet plane, soaring through the skies
A hero of middle earth that never seems to die
Not time or space can hold you back, there's nothing you can't do
You have power beyond belief and all the treasure too
The world is yours, the heavens too, to do with what you will
So live and love while you can until

The sun shines through your window and as you slowly wake
You realize it wasn't real, just a dream for goodness sake
But there's always another dream, when the sun is gone
And loves to love and lives to live better than your own

The problem though with dreams is that, if one ever does come true
You have to start all over within a day or two

So keep your feet firmly planted, while reaching for the stars
And all your dreams will come true, and the universe will be yours...

"Everyday Heroes"

August 11th, 2023

Here's to the everyday heroes
You know the people I mean
Those of you who work 24/7/365
Back behind the scenes

Those that care for their parents
Their own families as well
They sacrifice their own lives
And all they get in return is hell

Those who pick up the garbage
That would otherwise just pile up
And those who do the yard work
And keep the shrubs and the grass cut

Those who work in cafeterias
In the hospitals and the schools
Who keep our children and ill family fed
And they live by the Golden Rule

For the electricians and the plumbers
Who keep the power and the water on
And the folks who stop and help
Random strangers they happen upon

All those who give and support
Charities for children and animals too
It's people like you that keep
The world alive and on the move

For the carpenters and the builders
Who just will not sit still
While people are out in the cold
Until that last house is built

For the farmers and the ranchers
Who thank God are willing and able
Along with the truckers and grocers
Who keep the food on our tables

There are the preachers and the teachers
First responders and soldiers too
None of us would be even be here today
If it were not for all of you

All the single parents
Who bust their butts all day
To earn an honest living
And keep their children safe

To all of the grandparents
Who lend a helping hand
To raise that son or daughter
That not many understand

To all of those with special needs
That just want to be included
You have special gifts and talents to give
And that can't be discounted or disputed

There are millions of you out there
I cannot name all of you
Don't think you are invisible
Heroes one and all it's true...

Thanks to you all for everything you do!

"Fallen but not Forgotten"

July 19th, 2023

Today I visited a graveyard
Of soldiers dead and gone
And though they lie there stiff and cold
Their memories linger on

They fought for many reasons
And died for one and all
Some older and some much too young
To answer such a call

And as I walked amongst them
Lying there side by side
I read each name aloud
Then I began to cry

For I once served as they did
With honor and with pride
But for some unknown reason
God let me survive

So I'll try and tell their stories
All at once and with much despair
And share with you their glories
Of the soldiers who lie there

They came from near and far
And they made a mighty band
City lads and country boys
And shoulder to shoulder stand

They all stood for freedom
One branch or another
And prayed as one at each meal
And poked fun at each other

So camaraderie was born and bred
And they lived and died together
And they fought as one united
Now they lie here forever

No one was greater than the other
When they take their final bows
They will be united again
Up among the clouds

So if you ever wonder
What the cost of freedom is
Come here and just ponder
Where true sacrifice lives

And when you lay down at night
And in peace can dream
Just know that they stand guard
Over you and everything

Fallen but not forgotten
For through your thoughts they live
For all that you hold dear
Their lives they'd freely give

So this next holiday
While you're standing at your grill
Raise a toast to all those who went before To
those Elysian Fields!

"First Responders"

August 3rd, 2023

Today I knocked
On Heaven's Door
For God to let me in
Over on the Golden Shore

But God said to me;
"It's not your time my friend
I need for you to go back
And finish what you began."

I said; "But Lord,
I'm already here and yet
I've waited so very long
And I have no regrets."

"Child, you have not finished
Your mission that I gave
And there are many others
Whose lives you need to save."

"I need your talents and your skills
To spread more of my Grace
To all of those who without you
Would never see my face"

I cried; "I can see the streets of Heaven
Made of gold right over there
Haven't I been a faithful servant?
I don't think that this is fair."

"My precious little child I know
You do not comprehend
That the journey that I sent you on
Has not yet come to its end"

So, here I sit in the seat
Of my smoldering ambulance
And I can see that I am injured
With just one quick glance

You see I'm a paramedic
And many lives depend on me
But it's just not my time to go
I've so more to do and be

Even though I am hurting
Broken up inside
I get out and go to check
On the person with whom I did collide

There's a family of three
The parents are both okay
A father, mother, and a child
But the baby is beginning to fade

Then I take him from the car
And then I resuscitate
Using all my tools and skills
He's alive for goodness sake

Then I walk up to Heaven's Door
Then my God says to me;
"Welcome Home my child
Your mission is now complete."

So, I am walking down the streets of gold
Many people do I see
Whose lives had been extended
All because of me!!!

God Bless all our First Responders!!!
Angels without your Wings...

"Fond Memories"

July 31st, 2023

I have some fond memories
Running through my mind
Of a whole other world
And a better place in time

Of family gatherings
Down along the coast
At Granny and Pawpaw's place
Where we hung out the most

So many cousins and siblings
Running here and there
Chasing dogs and chickens
Never getting anywhere

Swimming in the river
Playing in the sun
Swinging from the rope
Having so much fun

Tag and Red Rover
Catch Me if You Can
Chase and Hide and Seek
Hey! No peeking man!

Riding bikes and pulling wagons
Down a red dirt and gravel road
Watermelons and sugar cane
Eating them all as we go

Catching lightning bugs
In an old fruit jar
Glowing in the dark
Out in the yard

Supper on the front porch
For all us kids and dogs
Fried chicken and sweet potatoes
Listening to the crickets and the frogs

Sleeping out under the stars
In sleeping bags and tents
Curled up with your dogs
Fire glowing softly in the pit

Good night from the Southland
Down on the farm
Fresh mown hay smells
Out from the barn

Fond memories all...

"For Rhyme & Reason"

August 25th, 2023

For rhyme and reason
From a poets point of view
Making music out of words
Is the thing I like to do

For rhyme and reason
From words to a song
How melodious are the lyrics
So, that you can sing along

Read everything with pleasure
Heed not to fits of rage
For words are just the music
That winds up on the page

So, for rhyme and reason
Making music into words
Isn't it the sweetest sound
Your heart has ever heard...

"From Here to There"

July 26th, 2023

How do you get from here to there?
Without going anywhere;
Pick up a book and turn the page
A brand new journey to engage
Buckle up and hunker down
You're about to leave this town
Using only your imagination
Anxiously and with anticipation
Chapter by chapter you journey on
Till pretty soon the night is gone
A few more hours and a thousand miles later
You shower down on the accelerator
Noon is just around the bend
You're quickly coming to the end
The plot thickens as you brace
The suspense has you frozen in your place
You're white knuckled and out of breath
Your heart is pounding in your chest
The climax has you near exhaustion
Now you must proceed with caution
The end is sudden and unexpected
Was there something that you neglected?
What the heck the story's through
It didn't end as you expected it to
Your journey is over
You turn the cover
And suddenly you realize
There's a sequel? That caught you by surprise!
You have to get it where's your phone?
That's another book to own
Another adventure that you must take
Another trip around the world to make
You're plum tuckered and worn out
And you haven't even left the couch

As you drift off you start to wonder
And you dream in your slumber
Then you wake with a shiver
Did Amazon just deliver?
There it is on the porch
You must read it now of course
Another journey on which you embark
On the bench down at the park

So, how do you get from here to there?
Without going anywhere;

I think you know the answer now
If you don't you'll figure it out somehow!!!

Bon Voyage!!!

"God didn't fail me"

August 14th, 2023

As I sit at my desk and try to write
Alone in the dark by candlelight
Words fail me

As I sit back and reminisce
To other times just like this
When words failed me

In times like these I started to pray
And never lacked the words to say
God didn't fail me

He gave me so much to be thankful for
So many people that I adore
And God hasn't failed me

So much time have I wasted
So much wine that I've tasted
But God didn't fail me

And as my tired eyes grow dim
I bow my head and worship him
My words pleased him

He never failed me in the past
So, I'll love him till at last
He brings me home to Glory
God never once failed me!!!

"Gods Rain of Love"

March 24th, 2015

Have you ever sat and watched?
As the rain comes falling down
How it cleanses all it touches,
Before it washes to the ground

It's more than just refreshing,
For there is life in its touch
It's just like the love of God,
That we need just as much

"Growing Old"

August 11th, 2023

"Old age isn't so bad when you consider
the alternative"... Maurice Chevalier

When we were little children
Growing old hardly mattered at all
As we got older it meant that we
Could stay out later if we called

Then there was a point in our lives
When our time was very tight
But there was also a time when
We could party all through the night

When we had to be in bed asleep by nine
Now we fall asleep just about anywhere
Growing old is a badge of honor
Displayed in our wrinkles and grey hair

But the time has just flown by
And we are wondering where it went
And as we sit here gray and old
We realize all of our time is spent

Our time here is getting short
Year-by-year and day-by-day
And we stare blankly out the window
Wondering how the time slipped away

So, if you are reading this
Take note and heed my advice
Do not waste a minute of time
Because it never happens twice

One day you will look around
And all your friends will be gone
And you will be one of the few
Left here to carry on

All you'll have are the memories
Go make them while you're young
So, you'll have something of your own
To look back on when your time is done

Growing old is a privilege
Granted to very few
So, live while you can
Before your life is through

Growing old with grace and vigor
Should be our personal quest
With our hearts and minds gifting love
Before we finally lay down to rest...

"Happy Heavenly Birthday"

August 4th, 2023

Happy Heavenly Birthday!
I wish you were still here
To celebrate this special day
That comes but once a year

You are still so very missed
And I wanted you to know
Just how much I love you
And I will never let you go

I honor you on this day
Year in and year out
Because in this way
There is never any doubt

You are forever in my heart
And always on my mind
You can still make me smile
Even after all this time

So, Happy Heavenly Birthday!
Enjoy it until the end
When I will join you there
And we'll be together again...

"Holding On"

August 20th, 2023

I remember when you were
Such a little tike
Learning how to walk
Was such a major hike

Furniture walking around the room
From coffee table to the couch
Until you got the courage up
To venture further out

I stood on the edge of the carpet
At the end of the hall
And when you waddled towards me
And you almost started to fall

But then you caught your balance
And came on anyway
Oh! How excited you were
I'll never forget that day

Then when you turned five
And got your first bike
And I taught you to ride
Down by the turnpike

"Please don't let go" you said
And I held you up until
You got your momentum
Then cruised on down the hill

I should have known it then
You'd only need me for so long
Because in no time at all
You were up and gone

You grew Oh! So quickly
That it was hard to see
The only one still holding on
Was me!

Then I blinked and you
Were all grown up and out
And off on your own
And I knew without a doubt

What a fine person
That you'd grown to be
And the only one still holding on
Was me!

But you were gone in an instant
Your time here had run out
Now I beat my fist against the wall
And I scream and shout

Now after all this time
I can plainly see
That the one still holding on
Is me!

I've got you baby
I'll never let you go
You're forever in my heart
And forever in my soul...

"Hope"

July 30th, 2023

I just wanted you to know
Just how make me feel
From just where I came
And that my love for you is real

I have spent so many
Long and lonely nights
Just clinging to the hope
That I would find someone so right

You have made my heart
Feel as light as a feather
And with You and God
I can stand any weather

This love that I feel inside
Is honest and it's true
And I know that now
It's all because of you ...

"How Long"
July 17th, 2023

How long must I go on hurting
And feeling the way that I do
Knowing that we're separated
By more than a breath or two

It seems as only yesterday
When we were oh so young
Now I'm growing old without you
And I feel like I don't belong

Counting the days one by one
And oh they seem so long
Surrounded by so many
Here in this world all alone

My mind it often wanders
Off down memory lane
And the times we spent together
Despite all of the pain

Oh, how I miss you
And I long for your touch
How I'd love to hold your hand
And kiss you oh so much

So, I just sit here thinking
About you night and day
And praying that I see you soon
Before you fade away!!!

"I Don't Remember"

August 17th, 2023

Every day is a brand new day for me
I can remember things from forty years ago
Like they were only yesterday
But what I had for breakfast I don't know

Or even what happened just the other day
Did I do this or did I do that and when
I don't remember what happened today
Let alone what happened then

So, please be patient
This is very upsetting to me
I was counting on my memories for when I grew old
I have very few of those now you see

Even my taste buds have no memory
Of the things I do and do not like to eat
I don't know if I will like it but
I guess I will try it, if I do then it's a treat

I don't remember if I have
Read this book before
Oh! Well it looks inviting
I think I'll read it once more

Please do not be angry
If I do not recognize
Certain things from yesterday
To me they are a surprise

I live with this daily
I hope you understand
I cannot help it
It's just the way I am...

"I Dream of You"

August 9th, 2023

When I was just a boy
I would dream of you
And had visions of grandeur
Of the things that we'd do

In my adolescence I wondered
Just when you'd come along
I even wrote about you
In the words of a song

But I knew the very moment
That that we first met
That you were the one
God made just for me, and yet

He made us wait a while
To learn to love and trust
Each other's feelings
And to control our lust

But we overcame
And now here we are
We have been around the world
In each other's arms

Somehow through time and space
You must have heard my plea
For when I wake each morning
You are lying next to me

And still to this day
Each and every night
I dream of you
When we turn out the light

So, do not for one moment
Think I do not care
For I worship and adore you
All the time and everywhere

And those times we are not together
And you are miles away
I look up at the moon
And I softly say

"Goodnight my love
Where ever you may be
When you close your eyes tonight
Please dream of me"

So, tonight when I'm fast asleep
After my prayers are said
"My Lord my soul to keep"
I will dream of you snuggled in my bed...

"I have Lost My Sun"

August 6th, 2023
(Excerpt from: "The Hardest Day")

They say the darkest hour
Is just before the dawn
But all day for me is darkness
Because I have lost my sun

My universe no longer
Has a center mass
To hold me and to warm me
And be a light unto my path

I just seem to be floating
Aimlessly lost in space
With no sense of purpose
Abandoned and disgraced

Time seems non-existent
No beginning and no end
Void of rhyme or reason
I'm unable to comprehend

The vastness of lonely
The emptiness of my heart
The deafening sound of silence
For your laughter will not impart

"I've Seen You in My Dreams"

May 16th, 2019

I've seen you in my dreams
You are often on my mind
You hold a special place it seems
In my heart all the time

When I close my eyes
I can see your face
It's like you are always near
In this cool and quiet place

No one has ever touched me
The way you used to do
I can't believe you're really gone
When in fact I know it's true

I want so very badly
To go back in time and say
I'm sorry for all the things I've done
That's driven you away

If I could have one wish come true
And know it would be done
I would ask to see you smile
Before the setting of the sun

You were the light of my life
For so very long
I am so lost without you now
And everything seems wrong

I am asking for your forgiveness
Before I start to fade
So that I might rest easier
When they lay me in my grave

So long to friends and family
And you my one and only love
May we meet again someday
In Heaven up above...

So here I am on Death's door
A heart full of regret
Ready to meet my Maker
And pay my final debt

"I Knew this Day was Coming"
December 10th, 2019

I knew this day was coming

I've known it for some time

That one day you would leave

Me and this world far behind

I wish I could have told you

Before you had to go

Just how very much I loved you

"I Love You"
September 3rd, 2023

"How do I say I love you"
"Let me count the ways"
Is one of life's most
Overused clichés

So, I'm going to try express
In so many different ways
How I say "I love you"
At least once every day

I washed a load of dishes
And dinner's on the stove
I did a load of laundry
And folded all the clothes

I swept and mopped the floors
Picked up all the Legos too
Cleaned up both of the bathrooms
And picked up the kids from school

Got the oil changed in the car
Ran an errand or two
Shopped for all the groceries
And laundry from the cleaners for you

So, if I forget to say the words
It's me you have to forgive
I've already showed you that I love you
In everything I did...

"I Thought of You"

September 2nd, 2023

I thought of you today
Like every day before
And every day that passes
I miss you even more

You are the best thing
That's ever happened to me
And the day you left this world
Was something I did not foresee

Now that you are gone
I feel hollow deep inside
Like an empty barrel
Busted open wide

Tears pour down daily
I cannot ebb the flow
The thought of you not here
Hurts more than you'll ever know

They say that with the passing of time
A broken heart will heal
After all these years
I don't think that it will

It hurts as much today
As it did the day you left
I feel as if I have been robbed
What a monumental theft

I know that by now
I should be back on my feet
But, I just can't somehow
I feel bound by defeat

Today is just a bridge
To get me to tomorrow
Maybe by then I'll be
Free of the guilt and sorrow

I cannot help but think
If it had been me instead of you
Things would be so much better
But, I don't know if that is true

Everyone has a time
To spend here on this earth
And when the sand runs out
It's the one's left who are hurt

For the ones who are taken
Will suffer here no more
They go on to Glory
To be with the Lord

All this I know and yet
The pain still lingers on
Every day is still a struggle
With the thought of you being gone

I thought of you today
Like every day before
And every day that passes
I miss you even more...

"Letting Go"
August 20th, 2023

I was taught to just hold on
From an early young age you know
Tightly to those things I wanted
Never letting go

After you came along
It was a boost to my ego
So I held on even tighter
Never ever letting go

As our love grew stronger
And my passion began to show
I looked forward to forever
And never letting go

The years flew by so quickly
And the winds of life did blow
And they took you away
I never dreamed of letting go

This rope that I'm holding onto
Has me swaying to and fro
Now I'm at the end
But I'm not letting go

Then you came from heaven
And in my ear whispered soft and low
"You must save yourself
The time has come for letting go"...

"Just Rambling"

July 26th, 2023

Lately I've been just rambling
About what all I think
Mindlessly wasting time
Paper and ink

So, please forgive me for just rambling
I don't mean any harm
With all the crazy things I write
While just pouring on the charm

I'm just having fun
Making this line rhyme with that
Pulling words from here and there
And from underneath my hat

But sometimes I can't sleep
So this is what I do
Making up little poems
Just for me and you

There are times however
When things are right on track
That I get on a roll
And I just don't look back

The words just seem to flow
Right out of my head
When I should be fast asleep
Snuggled in my bed

Or more often than not
I wake with such a start
With a great idea
That I have to impart

So bear with me for a moment
While I try to sort my thoughts
And put it down on paper
Before it all gets lost

I realize that I am just a hack
With no formal education
Just a man with paper and a pen
Writing to a lonely nation

There's a whole wide world out there
Of folks just like me
Who are hungry to impart
A bit of poetry

So pull up a chair or comfy couch
And sit for a little while
And listen to me rambling on
With a wry little smile

I may not be a writer
With a formal prose
But the words all dictate
When and where I go

What I'm trying to say is
This is how I feel
And I may not be perfect
But the words are just as real

I may not be a Longfellow
Or Ernest Hemingway
But I am just as sane
As they were I'd say

Edgar Allan Poe
May not be very proud
But the throbbing heart in my chest
Beats just as loud

So read on and I pray
That you will truly enjoy
The words I have to say
And the method I employ

Before I'm done and have to go
I hope you'll understand
What it is I have to show
To every person in the land

That I too was here
And I stayed for quite a spell
I had a few things to say
And a few stories to tell

I get a bit longwinded
But you ought to know
That is just the way I am
While I'm putting on a show

I've always been the clown
That makes everyone laugh out loud
While doing sometime stupid
For which I'm not very proud

I hope that I have outgrown
My old self of way back when
And I have matured a little
And can be more like a friend

Because I have changed
On my long hard journey
I feel like I am a better man
And not lying a gurney

In a morgue somewhere
Or maybe in a cell
Up to nothing good
That I did so well

So here I am just rambling on
About nothing important really
As a matter of fact
It all sounds kind of silly

But I digress
And move on down the line
And maybe to something better
On which to waste my time

So this is where I leave you
And I wish all the best
Of love and joy and peace
And much happiness

So long for now my friends
It's time for me to wake up
Make a pot of coffee
And fill a large cup

Drink it down black and sweet
Then get up and get going
Back to the work I love
Writing another poem...

"Kindly Give Me Back My Heart"

August 16th, 2023

Kindly give me back my heart
That you've broken right in two
So, that I can put it back together
And give it to someone new

You drug it through the streets
And down every dark alleyway
Ripping it all to shreds
Then you just threw it away

You never really wanted it
You were just being cruel
Now I want it back
Oh! I am such a fool!

You only wanted to keep me
As a trophy fling
I never mattered much to you
You are such an evil thing

So' now I want it back
So everyone will know
Just the type of person you are
You are all talk and no show

Thank you very much
And as you can plainly see
I have so much to do
Now please leave me be

So, now I have this broken heart
It's in need of some loving repair
Because a tender heart like mine
Is waiting for me alone somewhere...

"Lingering Love"

August 30th, 2023

Not a day goes by
That I don't think of you
There are many reminders
But, I don't know what to do

Time simply has no meaning
Now that you are gone
And I just merely exist
Like a bird without a song

It's not very often
I let someone get close
But, when I met you
I had really high hopes

You made my life worth living
You made all my dreams come true
But, you were gone so quickly
That I was torn right in two

So, now it's one night after another
Where I just cannot sleep
The thought of you being gone
Makes me tear up and start to weep

How long must I go on living
With you gone this way
My love isn't worth giving
I can't stand it one more day

My tears they fall like rain
From a thunderstruck sky
And I just cannot stop crying
I don't know the reason why

The memories of you haunt me daily
But, I cannot let them go
They are all I have left to cling to
And all I have to show

For years of love and trust
I gave my heart and soul
Although you are here no longer
I still love you so

So, I take a little siesta
To try and clear my mind
But, every time I close my eyes
Thoughts of you rewind

Sleep for me won't come
No matter what I do
Your lingering love still haunts me
And I still wake up missing you...

"Lonely Teardrops"
August 10th, 2023

My dearest love
This letter to you I write
To try and express my grief
Without you by my side

A hundred thousand feelings
Makeup just one tear
There are no words to say
How bad I want you here

The agony is horrendous
And there's just not enough
Medication in this world
To help keep my spirits up

It goes from a long slow ache
To a stabbing nauseating pain
And without you here with me
A smile I cannot maintain

I know that you had to go
And that you had no choice
I have been screaming at God
So loud that I've lost my voice

With all the evil people in this world
Why did he have to take you from me
What did I ever do that was so wrong
That he punished me so brutally

This life just doesn't seem fair
And I know I'm being selfish
But living without you here with me
Is a life that I do not relish

Now I have built a wall
Around my heart so broken
I'm afraid to let anyone get close
I cannot go through this again

So, I sit here daily weeping
In a puddle of lonely tears
Engulfed in unbearable emotions
Amidst all my doubts and fears

I feel so empty yet full of sorrow
That your life I could not save
For me there's no tomorrow
Without your love that I crave

I wish that I could be with you
And escape this awful place
There's no joy left for me here
If I cannot see your face

I've cried a million lonely teardrops
Since you have been gone
The pain of living without you
Has left me exhausted and withdrawn

So, I'll say goodbye for now
And seal it with a kiss
I hope that I'll get by somehow
And escape all this sadness...

"Love Light"
September 3rd, 2023

Remember this
When tough times come to call
These few words of wisdom
From a would be know it all

Time changes everything
Some things for the better
You've overcome things before
And stood in all kinds of weather

It's a learning experience
One that hurts like hell
Not always getting what you want
Often works out well

So, go ahead and have some fun
Do something for yourself
Be you own best medicine
Don't sit upon a shelf

Don't worry about other's negativity
It's not worth wasting your time
There's always something to be thankful for
So, let your love light shine...

"Love's Tender Pain"

August 27th, 2023

I didn't know true love
Until I saw your face
I didn't understand its meaning
Until I was wrapped in your embrace

The gentle way you took my hand
And held it Oh! So tight
And walked with me on the sand
Down on the beach that night

As we strolled together
Under a star filled sky
We shared each other's dreams
Until the sun was high

We lost all track of time
And miscounted the days
And I must have said "I love you"
A hundred different ways

And then the rain began to fall
And you had to hurry home
I never got your number
So, I could not telephone

I never knew how lonely
Alone could really be
Until you were not there
To keep me company

Three days along the shore
Does not a lifetime make
But, a lifetime of loneliness
Is not something I cannot take

So, as I gaze upon the moon
Way up in the sky
I wonder if you miss me too
On this long and lonely night

So, I lost your love
To the pouring rain
Now I understand
Love's tender pain...

"Man's Best Friend"

July 21st, 2023

We each need a friend
Someone who is loyal, proud, and true
Someone on whom we can rely
When we are feeling blue

Man's best friend is ready
And at your beck and call
Patiently waiting
To lend a friendly paw

They ask only to be loved
And treated oh-so-kind
And to know that you're coming back
When you leave them behind

They act as if you just left
No matter how long they have to wait
Anxious for your return
So be quick for goodness sake

So, if you have this special someone
That is present in your day
Consider yourself blessed
And loved in a special way

So after your long hard day
And you are homeward bound
Remember who's behind that door
Not just your ordinary hound

Man's best friend comes
In every shape and size
Some are just a handful
Some are gargantuized

Bundles of love they are
Wrapped up in fur and bone
But deep within your heart
They have found a home...

"Marriage"

August 1st, 2023

Imagine an institution so awesome
You want to check yourself in
And stay for the rest of your life
With your very best friend

I'm not saying things are always so rosy
There's times when you can't get along
But there's times when things are so right
Nothing can ever be that wrong

So, cherish your time together
Because you can never be too close
If you start to get on each other's nerves
Remember the vows that you chose

For richer or for poorer
In sickness and in health
Those are words to live by
And should not be put on a shelf

The secret to a lasting marriage
In my humble opinion is this
Try to out-love each other
And you will always experience bliss...

"Memories"

February 2, 2020

Softly drifting, gleaming dimly and silver lined
Reminiscing thoughts of another time

Snow white recollections of family and friends
Bringing smiles to my face again

Alone, seeking, and often find
In a special place in my mind

To hold close and very dear
So far away and yet so near

Years of wonder not surprising
A life full of compromising

Give and take here and there
Wisdom showing in my hair

So now I sit gray and old
So many stories left untold

Clear of vision and pure of heart
So much knowledge to impart

Of my life's secrets I hold the keys
Locked away with my memories

"Memory Lane"

July 19th, 2023

Tonight I wandered down Memory Lane
When an old friend I did meet
I cried inside as I remembered his name
As we were passing on the street

For he was bent, grey, and old
He did not recognize me
His eyes were glassy, hazed, and cold
And he could barely see

A cane he held in his hand
As he stumbled to a halt
A shell of the fellow he once was
And he stammered when he talked

"Do I know you he whispered?"
Through his straggly beard
And he strained hard to listen
His other hand to his ear

"It's me", I said just loud enough
So that he could understand
"It's been a while", I stated
And as I shook his haggard hand

"It's great to see you Sir"
As I looked into his face
I was searching for that twinkle
But I never saw a trace

He acted kind of desperate
As he tried to squeeze my hand
Like he wanted to remember
But just could not understand

"Just who are you?"
He cried in disbelief
Then waved me off and shook his head
As he staggered down the street

I stood there for a moment
A teardrop in my eye
And waited until he turned the corner
Then I softly said "Goodbye"

His name was Youth
And in his younger days
He had been quite the man
With his swagger and his ways

I knew him well for he was me
Now I ponder in my soul
And it's hard for me to see
That I too am getting old

So looking ever forward
I ambled down the Lane
To the place I was before
With my walking cane

Now I lay here all alone
And in slumber begin to dream
Of things I'll do before I'm gone
Could be most anything

As I doze, I begin to realize
There's not much time left for me
So, I start to prioritize
Then with the morning light I see

The time wasted dreaming
I could've gotten something done
So, now I sit here steaming
But just stay here in the sun

Then I start to think
Of fortunes I've won and lost
Of places that I've been
And the battles I have fought

Of people that I've met
And lives that I have lived
Of books that I have read
And knowledge I have to give

Remember there will be no doubt
When you meet yourself on the street
For when your time runs out
It'll be too late you'll see

Quit your dreaming
And start to do
All that you've been scheming
To yourself be true

So, if you ask for my advice
Here's what I have to say
Get up and go and live your life
Don't wait another day!!!

"Missing Dad"

July 21st, 2023

You know that you miss your dad
When you reach for your rod and reel
And you see at the back of the boat
That all is quiet and still

But you get this peaceful feeling
That he is sitting there
With his wise old eyes, and wry smile
And shock of blue grey hair

When you hear his voice in the breeze
"You're holding your mouth all wrong"
And when you cock your head to listen
Just like that he's gone

But you change the way
You hold your mouth and with a funny grin
You get a strike and set the hook
And reel the big bass in

Or you're sitting in your deer stand
You hear a big buck snort
Your hands begin to sweat
And you hear your Old Man's voice

"Easy on the trigger boy
And wait for him to relax
Aim just behind his shoulder blade
Then when you feel ready ...BANG"

Then off in the distance
You hear the coon dogs bay
And he slaps you on your back
As if to say

"They've got the ringtail treed
So gather up your get
And let's get on the trail
We'll have him in the burlap sack yet"

So many stories left untold
So many tales to tell
Of you and dad off on your own
On the lake or on the trail

Or even at the ball game
As the game drags on and on
A ballpark dog and a glass of beer
And the memories live on

Or at your last recital
When he cheered and clapped so loud
And embarrassed you and all your friends
But he was just so proud

Like when you first started racing cars
And he said that you were crazy
"But if you do it like this right here
You'll go faster than blazes"

So, even though you're missing Dad
His memory lives on and on
In all that you say and do
And in the words of this poem!!!

Love you Dad!!!

"Mister Monday"

July 31st, 2023

Monday is the most
Hated day of the week
But to me, it's a new beginning
And I find that quite unique

It's a chance to start all over
Now that yesterday is spent
When last week didn't end so well
Mondays are heaven sent

But sometimes we just feel
That two days is not enough
To rest and to recuperate
When the week has been to rough

What it is exactly that causes
Things to go all wrong
That we feel we have to fix
When Monday comes along

Maybe we just really need
To readjust and prioritize
The things that we are trying
Before the weekend arrives

But before you sound the alarm
And call the work police on me
Check your attitude at the door
And I will try and help you see

Sometimes it just takes
A few moments of your day
To stop what you're doing
And talk to God and say

"Lord help me understand
The when, and why, and where
Of things in my life that need
Your tender loving care"

I feel that if we can do this
At least once during the week
That we won't be so tired
That we feel we have to sleep

If we work as for the Lord
And pray each and every day
He will lead, guide, and direct us
All along the way

So, when the weekend rolls around
They'll be plenty of time to rest
And then Monday will not be so bad
Just give my theory a little test

And if you find you still have no time
To get everything you must do done
Then you can blame it all on me
I'll be on the beach soaking up the sun...

They call me Mister Monday!!!

"Mother's Day"

May 12th, 2023

Today is the day
We celebrate our mothers
She brought us into this world
And is unlike any other

They are all very unique
In their own special ways
Their little idiosyncrasies
In the things they do and say

Even though we set aside
This day to recognize
All of our mothers
Of every shape and size

We should really be doing this
Every single day of the year
Because they are the glue
That holds our families near

They conceived us in joy
Delivered us here in pain
They worry and they wonder
And they rarely ever complain

So, let's all gather around
And lift them up in prayer
Thanking God for this gift
Of mother's everywhere!!!

"Mother's Love"
January 18th, 2021

In love, you conceived me and carried me to term
In pain, you bore me another life's lesson learned
With tenderness, you nursed me and laid me down to bed
You bathed me and you changed me, from my feet to my head
And as the years wore on, you worked hard to help me grow
And be a man you could be proud of, from your heart and soul
From an early age you taught me, about the love of God
About the Holy of Holies, where the angels fear to trod
And how I could enter there, whenever I was feeling blue
To pray at the feet of Christ, like his disciples used to do
You gave me so much in life, and yet you're still giving today
I just want to show you, in every single way
Just how much I love you, for all you've said and done
For me, my spouse, my daughter and my sons

You epitomize the love of God, the very essence of Christ
May God Bless and Keep You

Thank You

"My Broken Heart"

August 16th, 2023

Shattered into a million pieces
Scattered near and far
Are all that I have left
Of my broken heart

Once proud and strong
It beat loud and with energy
Now it crumbles like a sand castle
When approached by the sea

I've tried to put them back together
But, I lack your loving touch
Now, I sit here in the darkness
Missing you so very much

Each and every night I pray
For guidance and for strength
For peace and for understanding
So that I don't sink

Deeper into the depths
Of depression and despair
So that I can begin to live
And to love and to care

I miss your loving kisses
And your soft caress
Your smile and your spirit
When I held you to my chest

It's hard to comprehend
Why you had to go
Knowing that I'd need you
And that I'd miss you so

So, sweep down from time to time
On your angel wings
And whisper softly in my ear
Sweet and lovely things

There will always be a place
For you here in my heart
I will keep your memory alive
And we will never be far apart...

"My Grandchildren, My Heart"

July 21st, 2023

To all of my grandchildren
I've loved you from the very start
From the moment of your first breath
You know you are my heart

A mother's love is sacred
This is very true
But a grandmother's love is special
You never can undo

There's no trouble that you face
That I don't know about
There's no problem or disgrace
That we can't workout

So bring all your heartaches
Your tribulations and your blues
And lay them on your grandma's lap
And I'll comfort you

You all are growing
So fast it's plain to see
Into fine the men and women
That you will someday be

I want you all to know
Just how proud I am of you
For all that you stand for
And all that you do

So here's some advice
Before you onward trod
Be true to yourselves
Your family and your God

And be you always faithful
To where and how you were raised
And never ever doubt
The Love that I gave

Know down in your heart of hearts
That I will always praise
The best of the best
That I have helped to raise

So go and do your duty
Stand proud and stand tall
And remember that
I love you one and all...

"My Heart"
August 9th, 2023

Please be careful with my heart
For it's as fragile as a flake of snow
And it may just melt away
From the warmth of your love's glow

I have never encountered
Someone with your touch
Who could move me as you do
With your tender words and such

You seem to really know me
Yet, we have only met just now
And I am beginning to wonder
When and why and how

Someone could so easily
Get underneath my skin
So surgically precise
And you my heart did win

Now as you take my hand
Gently into yours
I am starting to get the feeling
We have done this all before

Maybe, in another life
Long ago and far away
Now we are back together
And I hope that we can stay...

"My Salvation"

July 17th, 2023

When my heart is feeling heavy and my soul's a little blue
I get down on my knees and pray like Jesus said to do
I go into my garden and talk there with my God
For I have the right to go where angels fear to trod
He died there on the cross and took away my fears
And forgave me all my sins and wiped away my tears
He lifted all my burdens and healed my every pain
For He's the spotless Lamb of God and for my life was slain
So when I'm feeling weary and think I can't go on
I bow my head and thank the Lord for his Only Son
He bore my cross Golgotha bound and died there on that hill
And for me he rose again defeating Death and Hell
So, here I stand Victorious my life for Him I give
For I know it will be Glorious when at last with Him I live

"My Journey"

July 27th, 2023

I've been Heaven bound
For quite a while it seems
For I met Him as a child
Not yet in my teens

When I took Him as my Savior
I had no I idea of what I'd give
Where all He would take me
Or what kind of life that I would live

But I traveled onward
For many years I know
Closely to His Word
Because the Bible told me so

I studied on what He said
In His Word that was written down
All the letters in Red
As I traveled from town to town

Then somewhere I wandered
Off across the land
Led astray by my own desires
Far from the Master's plan

I committed nearly every sin
The Bible warned me of
And I found myself in trouble
Then I remembered about His Love

He had paid the price
For my sin and shame
I only had to repent
And call upon His name

So I sought His face
Down on y knees
And when I prayed
He heard all my pleas

And when I started listening
Very closely for His voice
I heard him say so softly
"Son, you have a choice"

You can either follow me
And eternal life you will gain
Or, you can go your own way
And live your life in vain

So, I followed him for a time
Until the road divided
Do I choose left or right?
I was so undecided

Then a voice over my shoulder said
"Take the road to the left
You will be happier with me
And you will have no regrets"

So I took the easy road
And left my God behind
Then I learned again
Of the trouble I would find

Oh! Lord what have I done?
There seems no way out
Then He said "I Am the One
To take away your fear and doubt"

So when I looked up
And considered my plight
I would take the right road
And follow Jesus Christ

And I can tell you now
I've strayed now and then
But He has never let me down
And He's closer than a friend

So, when you come to a fork
Or crossroads in your life
Never choose the left
Always choose the Right

This way is not as easy
It's rocky and it's rough
It's the road less traveled
But it's worth the long climb up

Sure the left road is wider
And a lot easier to follow
But it leads to a life of sin and shame
And in misery you'll wallow

Now I am far from perfect
And I still make mistakes
But when I call upon His name
He lifts me up for goodness sake

He never leaves or forsakes me
This I surely know
And His armor protects me
From Satan's fatal blows

So, my friends I will leave you
With this bit of advice
Always take the Right road
And follow Jesus Christ!!!

"Near"

July 17th, 2023

When the day is dark and dreary
And the clouds are sinking low
No ray of sunshine can be found
But there's one thing I know

Your memory it still warms me
And it brightens up my day
And it lightens up my path
So that I can find my way

I remember your sweet smile
And the twinkle in your eyes
Like it was only yesterday
And it caught me by surprise

The way you hugged me long and hard
Around my neck so tight
So that I can still sense your love
And it makes me feel just right

Even though you're gone
You are never very far
I can still see you in my mind
And I can feel you in my heart

"Night Wonder"
July 24th, 2023

Can you just imagine the wonder in their eyes?
Of those that came to see him first
And imagine their surprise
That from this swaddling baby
A new King would arise
To save them all from their sins
And give them eternal lives

And so I sit through space and time
And thousands of miles away
Just staring up at that same sky
That looked down on him that day

"No Mortal Creature Fair"

January 6th, 2020

No mortal creature fair doth measure up to you
With locks of golden sunshine and eyes of deepest blue
With skin as bronze as copper and velvet to the touch
And lips as sweet as honey which I crave way too much

A master's work of art on a canvas smooth and fine
Textures that are beyond compare by magical design
You speak to me in a foreign tongue intriguing to say the least
Unleashing desires within me I must beware the beast

For lust doth rip a man apart his heart from in his chest
His extremities grow weak and frail to breathe he does his best
How the Sirens of the ancient seas made the sailors wain
Such are the words to my ears that I cannot refrain

I am but a mortal no god's blood in my veins
So, I cannot withstand the torment and the strain
No Herculean strength can save me now
From the onslaught of your beauty so I before you bow

Be merciful to this lad as I am barely wet
Lacking knowledge and understanding of things I will regret
Your words cut so deeply through my armor made of steel
Straight through my heart and to my soul slay me as you will

But should I wake upon the Elysian field I'll know I did my best
In a war I could not win with a heart within my chest
For when love strikes one fairly dies a little every day
Although one strives to do what's right, he knows there is no way

So, love conquers all it has been said time and time again
But in the end, it is all you have until the Earth shall end
So, wage your wars and fight your fights though some will surely die
I choose love to do what's right till the by and by

"OLD SOLDIERS"

12/3/13

There is a place where I go to receive my healing
At the foot of an empty cross on Golgotha's Hill
And every time that I visit, there are others standing or kneeling,
Watching, waiting, and still.

They are all of the Old Soldiers, of battles lost and battles won
Yet they stand on like boulders, shoulder to shoulder waiting for God's only Son
They know that they do not have to stand there
For they have served their time, and have drawn their pay
But, still they stand, that marvelous band, with all eyes open toward Heaven
Just waiting and praying for that glorious day

They'll be standing there fearless in all their shining armor
When from the sky, the angel's trumpets blast
With swords and shields they'll salute with honor
When King Jesus comes again at last!!!

"Ole Summer Time"

July 18th, 2023

Many tales have been told
About Ole Summer Time
Of sweet corn picking
And Strawberry Hill wine
Swimming in the creek
When the work is all done
With siblings and cousins
Just having some fun
Of drive-in movies
On those sultry nights
And drag racing under
The interstate lights
Loud music a-blaring
In the Krystal parking lot
Rolling Skating at Skateland
When it got too hot
Fishing out on Big Creek Lake
For Catfish, Crappie, and Bass
Never mind that it's getting late
We'll leave right after this cast
Chasing lightning bugs
Out under the stars
Putting them into
Old glass Mason jars
The Good Ole Days
May all be gone
But in my memories
They still linger on
So here I go with one last line
Here's to Ole Summer Time

"On the Wings of a Dove"

August 8th, 2023

Yes I am in agony
My heart is broken in two
My life has been shattered
By the loss of you

What's left on me is scattered
All around from room to room
Each with its own memories
Which are hard to exhume

There are no words that I possess
For me to possibly proclaim
Just how much I really miss you
And I will never be the same

There is a hollow in my chest
Where you used to live
You've gone and left me empty
And there's nothing I wouldn't give

To hold you one more time
Run my fingers through your hair
Gaze into your eyes again
And say how much I care

You weren't here long enough
For me show you all my love
You just flew away from me
On the wings of a dove...

"One More Day"

July 22nd, 2023

One more day is all I need
To till the ground and plant the seed
To make amends where there's a need
Just one more day indeed...

One more day of guilt and sorrow
To buy, steal, beg, and borrow
To put off today and do tomorrow
Just one more day indeed...

One more day without the hail
To mow the hay and make the bale
To succeed where others fail
Just one more day indeed...

One more day of peace of mind
To write a letter or drop a line
To pay a bill without a fine
Just one more day indeed...

One more day to pay the rent
Even though the money's spent
To pay it down to every cent
Just one more day indeed...

One more day to get it done
To lay on the beach in the sun
Just so long as I'm having fun
Just one more day indeed...

One more day the bell to ring
To write a song about anything
To hear the choir begin to sing
Just one more day indeed...

One more day to steal a kiss
To hit the mark that others miss
To be someone they can't resist
Just one more day indeed...

One more day to stop and think
Do I really need this drink
To pour it down the kitchen sink
Just one more day indeed...

One more day to hit the brake
And slow it down for goodness sake
Be the one to give not take
Just one more day indeed...

One more day to ask Him in
And forgive me from a life of sin
Knowing that I alone can't win
Just one more day indeed...

One more day to breathe the air
And learn to say just when I care
So when heaven comes I will be there
Just one more day indeed...

Just one more day indeed...

"One of Those Days

September 3rd, 2023

It's been one of those days
When nothing goes quite right
And it continues on
Deep into the night

I stumble to the bed exhausted
From the labors of the day
Thinking about all the things
That got into my way

That kept me from doing
All I needed to
And took up all my time
That I wanted to spend with you

You are my reason for living
The highlight of my day
And it is hard to find
All the right words to say

I love you!!!

"One Smile Away"

August 25th, 2023

Who knows what tomorrow brings
It's the day after today
Something to look forward to
And, it's not so far away

It may bring joy and happiness
Or maybe sadness will abound
Who knows what tomorrow brings
But, it's there it will be found

Tomorrow never comes
I guess it's safe to say
Who knows what tomorrow brings
When it gets here it is today

So, don't worry about tomorrow
Think more about today
And all the love you've left to give
Is just one smile away...

"Pain in Hidden Places"

August 9th, 2023

I'm finding pain in hidden places
Since you have been gone
You left me with nothing to fight with
So, how am I to carry on

There's only darkness now
Where the light once dwelt
And only an aching in my heart
Like nothing I've ever felt

Why did you have to go
And leave me like you did
Wearing a frown now
Under a mask kept hid

I am putting on a charade
For those that do not know
Wearing a phony smile
So, the sadness doesn't show

How long can I keep on
Acting like I do
To keep the world from knowing
How much I'm missing you

Help me I beg you
Please hear my plea
Come from where you are
And heal this broken heart in me...

"Paw Paw"

July 28th, 2023

I wish that you were still around
To help me make bows and arrows
To take me fishing, and camping
And to keep me on my toes

And I wish that I could still walk with you
Through your garden picking
Okra, peppers, tomatoes, and corn
Seeing you start to sweat while you were
eating

Sitting me up on that milk stool
Showing me how to string line on a reel
Letting me sort your tackle box
Trying to get me to sit still

You kept me busy for hours
Doing this or that
Teaching me how to do things
Until it was time to take a nap

I recall the time
At the camp down on Old River
When you let me steer the boat
And I ran us up on the bank, remember?

You warned not to tell Maw Maw
For fear that she'd be upset
I wonder if she ever found out
But I will never forget

We caught so many catfish
On that ld trot line
That it tok us all night to clean
We got done way past nine

And you taught me to drive your tractor
To learn to mow the grass
And when Maw Maw had a fit
All you could do was laugh

"You're going get that baby hurt"
Was all that she had to say
But you still let me drive
And learned a lot that day

And when you sat me in your lap
And let me steer your truck
To distract me from where we were going
It was to your barber to get a crew cut

It never seem to fail every single summer
I would go to visit you
We would go get my haircut
It was the first thing you'd do

It made my mother mad
It made my father smile
But it really didn't matter
Because it grew back in just a little while

I wish that you were still here
To celebrate all our holidays
And to see your great-grandchildren grow
I wish that there was a way

We had so many adventures

That it's hard to remember them all
But most of them I'll never forget
Because we had a ball

Even though you are gone
I know that you can't be far
Because I have your memory
Right here in my heart...

"Perspectives"

July 25th, 2023

You know it's all about perspective
That certain point of view
That makes us all unique
In the things we say and do

Some of us are short
Others of us are tall
Some are kind of in between
With no idea at all

But we all look at things
From a different place
From a little different height
From a little different space

No two people are ever
Standing in the same shoes
So, we each report
A little different news

No two recollections
Are ever quite the same
Even though we might
Be playing the same game

So, do not be so quick
To condemn or to dismiss
People who are different
With a little different twist

And not be in such a hurry
To hate or criticize
Those who may not see things
As we see them through our eyes

Be careful what you call
The left wing or the right
Because we are all attached
To the same bird in our flight

Without both wings
An eagle could never soar
High above the landscape
Over the valley floor

It takes all kinds of people
From many different births
And from all walks of life
To make our lifestyle work

Like when you cook a meal
To feed your family
It takes all kinds of seasonings
For that perfect recipe

So, try to keep an open mind
When others are around
Not everyone is just like you
This I have easily found

This Nation can be
A wonderful group of states
Without all the derisions
That we've grown to hate

But if you keep God in mind
Whenever you make a stand
And Love your neighbor as yourself
And lend a helping hand

I am not saying to compromise
All that you believe
I am just saying do not wear
Your heart out on your sleeve

So, be proud of who you are
And what you want to be
Be true to your God
Your friends and family

Stand up for those who are too weak
To stand up for themselves
And do not be afraid to defend
This land you love so well

For if we stand united
Together straight and tall
We will never be divided
By anything at all

For in God we trust
And to Him we pray
That we live to see
Yet another day

So keep a good perspective
When you travel from place to place
And experience the differences
That make us The United States...

"Poetry is Music of the Soul"

August 19th, 2023

"What makes you want to write poetry?"
Someone once asked me
"What do you hope to accomplish?"
And I responded pointedly

Poetry is
Music of the Soul
It is just as powerful
As your Rock & Roll

It often moves people
A little differently
With a lot of emotion
In perfect harmony

It may or may not rhyme
Or even be very long
And it can be used as
The words to a song

Poetry can move
A person's spirit
And if you listen close
You can even hear it

Even King David
He of Biblical fame
Was a mighty poet
And author of the same

From Longfellow to Tennyson
Even many more
Were mighty men of words
As well as that of war

Dickinson and Brooks
Teasdale and Browning too
Were great women of words
Just to name a few

I hope that long after
I am dead and gone
These words that I write
Will continue to live on

In the hearts and souls
Of the lonely and the lost
To recite on some dismal day
When they are tired and be tossed

So, when you are down
And feeling sick and blue
Recite a few lines of poetry
And you'll feel renewed

Poetry often happens
When two worlds collide
Welling up emotions
You've kept locked deep inside

So, sit back and grab a pen
And a sheet of paper or two
And listen to your heart
And you'll write poetry too!!!

"Positivity"
September 3rd, 2023

Thinking positively
About all things bad or good
Can change your whole point of view
So, they work out like they should

So, just keep on trying
Even if you fail the test
If you learn anything at all
Next time you do your best

Success isn't a destination
But a journey for goodness sake
Consider it a lesson learned
With every step you take

Positivity is contagious
It jumps from one to another
Soon it's an epidemic
That we spread to each other

So, go ahead and smile
What harm can it do
It is one disease
I'd love to catch from you

Go ahead and spread it
To every person that you meet
Even people you don't know
Will appreciate the treat...

"Questions"

August 16th, 2023

So many questions left unanswered,
As to why you had to leave.
So much time on my hands,
For me to reflect and grieve.

Why did you have to leave me?
Was it something I did or said?
I need to know the answers,
Before I can rest my head.

You left so very suddenly,
I didn't get to say goodbye.
And the questions left unanswered,
Are still burning in my mind.

Since you've been gone
All I've done is mourn
Not sure what else to do
I feel lost and so forlorn

The tears are falling hard
Streaking down my face
I am so broken hearted
Helpless and disgraced

Nighttime brings no comfort
I toss and turn and cannot sleep
So, I just walk the floor
With no shoes on my feet

My head is pounding fervently
And my tears fall like the rain
My mind is numb and racing
My body trembles with the pain

Alas the morning sun
Breaks through the stormy sky
But still you are not here
And my question is just, "Why?"

Then the door swings wide open
I see you standing there
I can't believe my eyes
You just appeared out of thin air

We rush into each other's arms
And hold each other tight
So many questions still unanswered
But for now it's all alright...

"Remember, when you are down and out"

August 16th, 2023

Remember, when you are down and out
There are others in that same boat
When the storms of life toss you about
The love of God keeps it afloat
So, take his hand and he'll calm the sea
And make everything alright
And soon enough if you believe
You too will see the light...

"Shooting Star"

December 6th, 2020

I wished upon a shooting star as it raced across the sky tonight
And I wondered just where you are and if you were alright
Because, it's been so very long since I held you in my arms
And listened to your secrets as you worked your magic charms

I hope that you are safe and sound as you journey on your trip
Out upon life's oceans in your majestic little ship
I know you said you needed space and time to clear your mind
I just pray you don't forget me as yourself you begin to find

I know that you had to go away and yet I wonder still
Did you leave on your own or was it just the chill?
Of the ice within me that will never melt
Until you hold me close again with a fire, I've hardly felt

So, as you journey on your way and step from star to star
Look back upon where you've been so you'll know just where you are
And I will keep a bright light burning here so that you can see
Across space and time, the way right back to me

Come back and melt my cold, cold heart and warm my frosty mind
So that I can show you a soul mate you will find
Tonight, I saw a shooting star and it reminded me of you
Of all the good times we had and of the love that we once knew

"Someday"

August 14th, 2023

Someday I would like to soar
Like the mighty eagle flies
Away up above the clouds
In the bluest of the skies

Then swoop down
At breakneck speed
To the earth below
Oh! To be wild and free

To experience the exhilaration
Feel the blood rushing through my veins
Know the excitement of adventure
Just to be alive again

But for now I just sit here
Embalmed to the gills with meds
Staring blankly out of my window
Waiting to be pronounced dead

I might as well be gone
I serve no earthly purpose
I'm just taking up space
I'm completely out of service

Someday soon I hope
I'll pass on from this world
And be in a better place
In a new body impearled

Someday I'll walk upon
The golden streets so bright
And I will in chorus sing
To the angels pure delight

Someday come and visit
And see me before I pass
It won't be long before
I will be at peace at last

Someday

...

"Sometimes I Sit and Write"

July 20th, 2023

Sometimes I sit and write, for hours at a time
About nothing in particular, just whatever's on my mind
Maybe about something, that happened just today
Or something that happened years ago, long ago and far away

Perhaps about the news, that I so dislike
That seems to haunt the TV, both day and night
The talking heads my doctor warned me, will make you go insane
If you watch too much he said, you've only yourself to blame

Some things I really need to know, about most I do not care
Just the facts and nothing more, about who, what, when, why, and where
I like to make the words all rhythm, as often as I can
But sometimes it does not happen just the way I plan

So please forgive me, for having a bit of fun
For the words just keep on coming, and cannot be undone
So I sit here and write, a little selfishly
But it is such a delight if not a bit shamelessly...

"Sometimes"

August 14th, 2023

Sometimes I feel so lost
Empty and alone
Wandering aimlessly
No place to call my own

Sometimes I think that I
Am dying more every day
And soon I will disappear
Just up and fade away

Sometimes I wonder
What life must be like
To experience love and joy
Morning, noon, and night

All I have known is pain
Each and every day
I go life complaining
So tired and full of dismay

What is it really like
Over on the other side
How I would love to go
Across the great divide

Sometimes I imagine
A place of pure bliss
That knows no sorrow
Opposite of all of this

I guess that I am doomed
To just forever abide
Washing back and forth like the sea
coming in and back out with the tide

Sometimes I wish upon a star
Streaking across the night sky
Asking of the possibilities
That I could catch a ride

Sometimes...

"Song of the Cicada"

September 3rd, 2023

Have you ever heard
The song cicada sing
It lulls you to sleep at night
With its repetitious ring

Isn't it amazing
How real nature is
That something so seemingly ugly
Can make music such as his

Ugly is only skin-deep
Despite what people say
Caterpillars turn into butterflies
Every single day

People who look for ugly
Only ugly will they find
But, people who look for beauty
Will find it every time...

"Sounds of the Night"

August 19th, 2023

Have you ever listened
To the sounds of the night
Of the crickets, cicadas, and frogs
From well before dark till the morning light
A symphony of the forests, fields, and bogs

It's music for the soul
A free concert for all to hear
It's a song that never gets old
No matter whether you are far or near
So, find a seat, listen close, and you too will behold

As the evening sun sets
All the stars start to come out
And the moon takes its place in the sky
All of the night creatures start to stir about
And the chorus begins to sing the sounds of the night...

"Summer Moon"

July 31st, 2023

Summer moon so big and bright
Lights up the southern sky
Moving oceans and making waves
Sing me a midnight lullaby

How often have I gazed
Up at your beauty deep
Until you sink into the sea
And I fall fast asleep

You just seem to hang there
Lonely in the dark
Even though there's billions
Of other giant twinkling stars

They're dwarfed by your light
As they are very far
Supernovas they may be
But I know who you are

You are the keeper of the night
Watching over me
Right up to the daytime
When the sun I will see

So rock me slowly softly
In the cradle of your glow
And sing a song so lofty
That it heals the mortal soul

My words do not do justice
To majesty of your face
But you are the master
And my saving grace

Sometime I'd like to visit
And sit upon your crest
While you whisper lowly
And the meaning of love express

So, good day summer moon
And until tomorrow night
When you circle round again
And enchant me with your light...

"Sunrise & Sunset"

July 19th, 2023

My two favorite times of day
Are Sunrise and Sunset
The Alpha and Omega
The beginning and the end

Each with a special meaning
I will explain it to you my friends
God needed a place to start
So, he created the sunrise

Something that was so beautiful
You're bound give Him praise
When you open up your eyes
Thankful for another day

You see a new day dawning
Brand new opportunities

And great possibilities

"Take My Hand"

July 29th, 2023

Take my hand and walk with me
Way down by the salty sea
Hand in hand along the shore
Listen to the breakers roar

Finding treasures aren't they cool
Wading in a tidal pool
Sand up between your toes
Watch the way the current flows

Waves crashing on the beach
Sand crabs scurry out of reach
The tide slips in and swirls about
Seaweed stinks there's no doubt

Seagulls squawking overhead
Pickets in the dunes ahead
Salt grass waving in the breeze
The sun is setting into the sea

A full moon rises in a brassy sky
Crimson clouds go drifting by
Shadows appear here and there
Night time smells of salty air

On the point the lighthouse glows
Beams of light the ships to show
The way into the harbor docks
So they don't run up on the jetty's rocks

Night comes softly creeping
Stars glowing and lightly twinkling
Time's slow and slightly sleeping
Moon's guarding silently keeping

We can stay awake no more
Goodnight from the sea shore...

"Thank You for Your Service"

August 28th, 2023

"Thank you for your service"
I have heard quite a bit lately
"You are quite welcome" I reply
Feeling somewhat stately

It really was my pleasure
To have the privilege to serve
In the military service
Both active duty and reserves

It was a job like no other
That I've had before or since
One that I'd gladly do again
If that makes any sense

You see, there was camaraderie
That we all once shared
A friendship based on trust
That just does not compare

So, for all you young people
Looking for a place to start
Why not join the service
And give it all your heart

Then one day when you are older
You'll look back and say
I was proud to serve my country
And I'd do it again today

So, for all of you who have served
It would be a great disservice
If our nation didn't say
   "Thank You for Your Service!!!"

"The Beach"

July 26th, 2023

If you ever find
That you really need
A little break from life
The Beach is the place to be

Try to start out
Early in the morning
And watch the sun come up
With a brand new day dawning

The soft comfort of
The waves slowly coming in
And the calls of the seagulls
Floating on the wind

Finding the treasures
That washed up on the shore
You know they've been in hiding
Down on the ocean floor

And the tiny little creatures
That scurries on the sand
Looking for a morsel
Of food where they can

They dart to and fro
Trying hard to stay
Away from the other beachcombers
That might get in the way

And as the waves
Steadily stronger get
You will find it hard
To keep from getting wet

As the day progresses
And the sun gets high
You will notice that
There's hardly a cloud in the sky

Then along towards
The lazy afternoon
You will see on the horizon
The outline of the moon

Then in the evening
As the sun is slowly sinking
Into the ocean surface
You get this awesome feeling

You think to yourself
Man! This is the life
Free from all the hustle
And bustle and the strife

Then when the moon
Has risen high
You start wonder
How it affects the tide

When you suddenly notice
The subtle changes in your mood
How you went from all stressed out
To feeling really good

So, there you have it
Life at the beach is so sublime
Now if you could just afford
To stay here all the time

But don't forget
You're just a ride away
From that peaceful easy feeling
That you deserve every day!!!

"The Christian Soldier"

August 15th, 2023

Many a war has been waged
With many battles fought
Many lives have been saved
But millions have been lost

And the Christian Soldier
Has marched to the tune
In every major battle
That history can exhume

Many have fought for freedom
Many more have met their fate
Some have gone on to Glory
And walked thru the Pearly Gates

But the Christian Soldier
Has carried the cross with valor
And waged war on the devil
And his minions they did shatter

Crusaders they were called
927 years ago to the day
Off to fight for freedom
In the first of the Crusades

So, "Onward Christian Soldier
Marching off to war
With the cross of Jesus
Going on before"...

"The Code Talker"

July 27th, 2023

Very often I am faced
With such an dark topic
And I can't help but wish
That I could physically stop it

The subject matter is that of
Death around the corner
And helping family deal with it
Instead of being just a mourner

Many years ago
A long time in the past
I had to conduct a funeral service
For a church member who had passed

I did not know him very well
For he had been ill for a long time
And had not been there
To a service of mine

So, before the day came
To lay his soul to rest
I did a little research
And put my skills to the test

I found that this man of God
Who had been loved by everyone
Had once been a code talker
In the Army during World War One

Now I was just a young man
Fresh out of the Air Force
So, I was pretty impressed
By his history of course

A great soldier among his troop
And had several times over
Shown what he could do

A member of the Choctaw Tribe
It seems as if he had been
Drafted by the US Army
To fight in the War way back then

Now the story of these brave men
Is known far and wide
How they used their native tongue
To ultimately stem the tide

Of the German Army
Wreaking havoc across the front
Creating codes that could not be broken
By any enemy grunt

These men and their language
That was unknown across the seas
Fought the enemies they faced
And brought them to their knees

This went on for the duration
Of that awful war
And the service of these great men
Caused a turning point for sure

They were not highly decorated
For their heroics there at the end
But later on after many years
They were recognized by Uncle Sam

Then a long time later
A book was written and a movie made
About these men of Valor
These American Indian Braves

Finally, in 2001
After many years in red tape spent
These brave men were honored
By a United States President

They were given golden Medals of Honor
For their Valor and their skills
From a grateful nation
And this gave me chills

And even though the honors
Were given so very late
And their lives were nearly over
They could still appreciate

Their stories go to show
What goes on behind the lines
That sometimes really great people
Just have to bide their time

Just like being a humble Christian
Patience comes into play
Knowing that our Savior
Will recognize us on that Great Day

So, go rest in peace Great Warrior
You can now be found
Living with your God forever
In the Happy Hunting Grounds!!!

"The Days of My Innocence"

August 28th, 2023

Take me back to my childhood
Before I learned to dread
To the innocence of my past
Please, before I am dead

But, to go back to my childhood
Of which I often dream
Would be so magnificent
Just to play, shout, and scream

Oh! The joys of childhood
Please Lord take me there
To the days of my innocence
When I did not have a care

Chasing down the ice cream truck
Drinking from the hose
Playing in the sprinklers
Riding bicycles down the road

Catching fireflies and swinging
Oh! So very high
Then jumping out on your way up
And soaring through the sky

Even on days when it would pour
We'd play out in the rain
Splashing in the puddles
I'd love to do that again

So, I'll put those on my bucket list
Of things to do before I pass
When I walk through those Pearly Gates
I will be at peace at last...

"The Golden Years"

July 28th, 2023

"The only thing worse than growing old is never getting
the opportunity"

I've finally reached the Golden Years
Where I said I'd never be
And I sit teary eyed
Because my friends aren't here with me

Most of them are dead and gone
But their memories still live
So, I sit here reminiscing
What have I left to give?

Separated by time and space
People come and go
I find it's hard you see
In this place I do not know

Nurses come in and out
With my meds and supplements
You know I appreciate them
They must be Heaven sent

I think I'll go for a walk
Down the hall to see
Maybe even stop to chat
With someone that I meet

This place is not familiar
Where am I today
You think that would know
But it's hard to say

Here I am in room full of folks
Playing games and such
Maybe I can get in on one
I don't do this very much

Checkers, chess, and dominoes
Are all that I can recall
So with a cup of coffee
I sit down with them all

I feel all alone
In this little crowd
But I play anyway
I'll get along somehow

As we play on
I'm thinking that I'd like
To win a round or two
And then I do, what a delight

Along about then
They start to bring
Dinner for us all
I'm hungry for anything

Baked chicken and sweet potatoes
Green beans and Jell-O too
It all looks so tasty
It must be comfort food

After dinner around 6 o'clock
They turn on the big TV screen
It's an old western movie
One I've often seen

Where the hero
Always seems to get
The girl he loves and then
They ride off into the sunset

Well what a way to go
That sounds good to me
And then later on
As I drift off to sleep

I dream a cowboy's dream
Where I'm the hero and have no fears
And I ride off with the sunset
Into the Golden Years...

"The Hardest Day"

August 5th, 2023

Today has been the hardest day
Because you were nowhere near
And though I listened to every sound
Your voice I did not hear

How can I continue
To carry on this way
If every moment from now on
Is going to hurt like it did today

The pain I feel consumes me
And I cannot seem to make it ease
My heart is heavy with sadness
So, I'm down here on my knees

Praying for peace and understanding
Wondering what I might have done
To cause the Lord to punish me
And my soul to shun

I'm not sure of the reasons
For your untimely demise
I just feel so cheated
As the tears fill my eyes

There's a place in my chest that's empty
And can never really be filled
A void in my life that's left me
Feeling all alone and still

They say the darkest hour
Is just before the dawn
But all day for me is darkness
Because I have lost my sun

My universe no longer
Has a center mass
To hold me and to warm me
And be a light unto my path

I just seem to be floating
Aimlessly lost in space
With no sense of purpose
Abandoned and disgraced

Time seems non-existent
No beginning and no end
Void of rhyme or reason
I'm unable to comprehend

The vastness of lonely
The emptiness of my heart
The deafening sound of silence
For your laughter will not impart

So, now I'm drifting away
Fading from the light
Into the depths of darkness
To the everlasting night
Your death has stolen my life...

"The Key"

September 3rd, 2023

You hold the key to my happiness
You hold the key to my heart
You've held all my attention
Right from the very start

You are the key to my past
And my future too
And I would be so lost
If it were not for you

My love is locked away
Deep inside of me
Only you can unlock my love
For you alone hold the key...

"The Legend of the Dogwood"

August 10th, 2023

There is a famous legend
Of the Dogwood Tree
One that bears retelling
So that everyone can see

The story goes that the tree
Was once mighty, tall, and strait
But after the crucifixion of Christ
God forever changed its fate

It is said that this is the tree
That bore the Savior as a cross
To save us all from our sins
So, we would not be forever lost

The legend says that the tree
Was both cursed and blessed
With thin and crooked limbs
And a flower unlike the rest

Thin and crooked so that it would
Never again bear the weight
Of someone to die again
On a cross for Salvation's sake

But blessed with a blossom that
Is in the shape of a cross so nice
With nail prints and a crown of thorns
That represents that great sacrifice

So, when you a Dogwood tree
Growing on the side of a hill
Remember that Great Sacrifice
Christ died doing his Father's Will

Salvation isn't free
But it was paid in full that day
By Christ Jesus on the tree
So that we can always say;

"I am saved from my sins
By the Blood of Christ
And forever I can have
A blessed eternal life"...

"For God so loved the world, that he gave his
only begotten Son, that whosoever believeth
in him should not perish, but have everlasting
life" John 3:16 (KJV)

Amen!!!

"The Light"

August 1st, 2023

I saw the light shining through the darkness
On a stormy sea tempest tossed and distressed
From a lighthouse upon the shore
And I knew then that I had been truly blessed

When I ventured forth in life to make my living
And this happened many times as I traveled the sea
I prayed and asked God for deliverance
And every time He shined his light on me

So, whenever you find yourself lost
And tossed on stormy seas
Remember to seek God's face
And he will grant you peace...

"The Meaning of Life"

August 21st, 2023

Have you ever wondered
What's it all really worth
The time spent till now
From the moment of you birth

All of the aggravation
The blood, sweat, and tears
The cursing and the yelling
Down through the years

Like when a simple project
Turns into an awful mess
Then you come all unglued
Ultimately failing the test

You see, life is a series
Of ups and downs
Of little life lessons
On which to expound

We've many examples
Down through history
Of who to be like
Or not to be

I've often pondered
The meaning of life
So, I researched the answer
Till deep in the night

And this is what I found
Life is a quality of existence
To experience change till death
And we are not here by happenstance

We all have a purpose
To fulfill before we die
A goal in life to accomplish
So, find out just what and why

To give back better than we received
For those who will come along after
To love and to learn and to grow
As was the plan of the Master

So, I've made a determination
For me and for no one other
I will serve the Lord
Just as I will love my brother

"The Moon"

July 19th, 2023

How bright is the moon?
On a dark and lonely night
When everything's a mystery
Bathed in its amber light

But out upon the water
Its ripples all aglow
The tiny waves in motion
As they dance to and fro

But out in the forest
The woodland's fast asleep
Except for the wise old owl
Who's faithful watch he keeps

Out upon the prairie
As the winds softly blow
The tall grass gently waves
And its blades softly glow

So, it's all about perspective
What you can and cannot see
But a slight change here and there
Could be the remedy

So do not fear the darkness
Nor any man or beast
Just change the way you look at things
And there you'll find your peace!!!

"The Medical Professionals and the Nurses"

July 27th, 2023

To all the Medical Professionals and the
Nurses
Who bust their chops both day and night
Doing all the good things they do
To help in saving people's lives

Their jobs are never easy
And they seldom get to rest
They spend all their time
Giving meds and performing tests

And countless other things
That never gets recognized
They're getting spit, bled, and peed on
And often scrutinized

Their families also suffer from lack of their
attention
All their children, and husbands, and wives
And they rarely get to take vacations
To help recharge their own lives

As a former patient
Who's been on the brink of death
More times than I can count
I just want to tell you now before I'm out of
breath

How much you are worth to me
And how much I really care
For everything you've ever done
While I was a patient there

There are so many of us
Who know and appreciate
All the things that you do to keep us
Outside the cemetery gates

There are so many others
Who just don't give a damn
Who think that it's just your job
But that's not who I am

You people are vitally important members
Of our daily lives
For we could not really function
If you weren't by our sides

So, I just want to thank you
From the bottom of my heart
And because of you I am alive
And I have been given a brand new start

For all those other people
Who really just do not know
I thought that I would write this poem
So that I can show

The work that you all perform
The studying that have to do
Just to stay abreast
Of what is expected of you

And I'm grateful for you every single day
Because after two strokes, heart attacks, and
stints
I'm lucky to even be alive to say
You all must be Heaven sent

So, please just hang in there
Even for a little while
Because you are best
And we need your friendly smile

So, God bless you and keep you
Very close to His heart
Because there's whole world out there that
needs you
And the care that you impart... 🖤

"The Men Among Us"

July 20th, 2023

To all the men among us
We thank you one and all
For standing up to be counted
Chest out, proud, and tall

Men of God tried and true
Of integrity and grace
Kind of heart, and full of love
Honor and of praise

Men who can hold a baby
As gentle as a lamb
But who can be as hard as nails
When the times demand

Those who seek peace and wisdom
At the throne of God
And who are not afraid to go
Where angels fear to trod

Silently in prayer
Down on your knees
Not boisterous or loud
In questionable company

We lift you up and hold you close
An example we all need
For you are the ones we chose
To gently take the lead

So if you are that kind of man
We salute you one and all
Doesn't matter what your stature is
You're the greatest of us all

So, we give thanks to God above
For all the men like you
And all we ask is that you keep
Doing what you do...

"The Morning After"

September 1st, 2023

The morning after yesterday
Is the worst by far
Because I have yet another day
To wonder where you are

The pain of losing you gets worse
With every passing day
I don't know how much longer
I can continue on this way

I know you're in a better place
And that's just fine for you
But, I'm not in very good shape
With all I'm going through

I know that I'm being selfish
I've heard all that before
It's just that I love you so
And, I can't handle any more

So, if you could show me
Just a little sign
Something so that I can know
That I will be just fine

I'm walking in the darkness
And I need a light
My eyes are red and bloodshot
I know I look a fright

But this is how it's been
Since you have been gone
I don't go out in public
And, I don't talk on the phone

I don't have much to say
To make others understand
I don't know how to handle this
But, it is not what I had planned

Facing a new day
Is something that I dread
With curtains drawn
I lay aching in my bed

People handle grief
Differently I am told
Some withdraw like I do
Some act all big and bold

Everyone's path is different
No one's quite the same
I just wish I could understand
And get back in the game

So, please be patient
While I try and work this out
And you'll have to forgive me
If I scream and shout

They say time is the great physician
Healing all, bye and bye
But, it seems to take forever
And, all I can do is cry...

"The Morning Sun"

August 1st, 2023

As the morning sun comes peeking
Over the rooftops and the trees
It begins to brighten up the sky
And warm the morning breeze

As I sit here contemplating
All that I need to do
With my first cup of coffee
As sunlight sparkles on the dew

Then the rooster crows
That it is now the time
To get up and get going
And try and make a dime

The day will not be as peaceful
As it is right here and now
With all the birds and squirrels stirring
But I'll make it through somehow

So, I bow my head and give thanks
For yet another beautiful day
To be all I can possibly be
In each and every way... Amen!!!

"The Poet"

August 23, 2018

I slumber naught till morning light
When golden rays shall come
And bath me in its glory bright
Till another day is done

From far across the oceans
And over the mountain glade
It rocks me with its motions
While I dream the day away

When at last my eyes shall see
The setting of the sun
As the dusk drifts over me
And another night begun

So, I reach for my pen
To write yet another line
And tell a tale for you my friends
So comfort you may find

From words and rhymes
Through pen and ink
Down the hallways of my mind
I'm lost in what I think

I struggle now and then
With what I want to say
And never really know just when
They fall just where they may

So, I toil the long night through
While many others doze
With pen and paper just for you
This song that I compose

So, read on my friends
And in tempo keep
Because when the song shall end
I'll be fast asleep

And as I leave you pondering
About how I lived and died
I started off just wandering
And floating with the tide

Till one day a book I'd find
With writing, oh so sweet
How the words did rhythm
And with penmanship so neat

I promised on that day
And by the pale moonlight
If nothing but a single phrase

That I would surely write...

"The Rolling Thunder"

July 26th, 2023

Many songs have been written
About the Rolling Thunder
But how many of us really know
What's going on up yonder

Sometimes when it's storming
And the thunder begins to roll
I just sit and listen
For its fury to unfold

When the clouds begin to march
Across the southern sky
And the rain begins to fall
From way up on high

Then the lightning flashes
Way too close it seems
And the windows rattle
From back behind the screens

Then after several seconds
The Rolling Thunder sounds
From deep within its bosom
Rumbling through the town

This goes on and on
Till the storm passes by
And all the clouds roll back
To reveal a brassy sky

Then off in the distance
Just as if to boldly say
Thanks for your attention
I'll be back another day...

The Song of Grey Wolf

5/17/2019

Born to run within the pack, a pup of Nobel blood
He grows to adulthood, as any fighter should
He learns the value and the lifestyle of the vicious clan
Gaining in strength and in cunning as he roams across the land
Keeping all within the sight of his blue-grey eyes
Lest he fall from weakness and his untimely demise

Now he entered adolescence knowing all to say the least
As a cocky robust loner and unsavory hateful beast
He followed the herd from mountain high to valley low
Taking what he wanted from those that were too slow
Feared by all the others as he traveled on his way
Living off the land taking what he may

Then came the time he chanced upon an older, weaker king
And struck him down and took his throne and his following
So now he is in his own high and rightful place
And leads the pack on the hunt, a never-ending race
They strike quick and often, no mercy in this band
For he is their heart and soul on this trek across the land

He reigns on high for a time no one to challenge him
Until one day he flounders, and his eyes grow dim
A strapping youth comes forth looking to make a name
Defeats the older leader and his spot does rightly claim
Now he is ousted as their king and he has not the strength to try
They banish him from their midst and leave him there to die

Now old and nearly blind he wanders, waiting for death to come
For there is no one to lead or place he can call home
So high upon the mountain he makes his final stand
And looks out upon the vastness of the empty lonely land
His time on earth is over, death knocks upon his door
Life has come full circle, Grey Wolf is no more

"The Stormflower"

August 14th, 2023

As the storm raged the flower bloomed
And love rode wild across the plain
Lightning flashed and the thunder rolled
The Stormflower was born in the driving rain

"The Teachers"

July 31st, 2023

This is for all the teachers
Who have ever stood in front of a room
And have given away their knowledge
For a lot less than one might assume

Now I am not asking anything from you
And I'm not looking for a passing grade
I just wanted to write and tell you
You're the reason I write poetry today

And to thank you for all that you say and do
I know it's not the easiest job that you've had
You wish on some days you could retire early
Because I am that kid that you thought was bad

I really have to tell you now
To please just hang on
Because there are children
Who need you to lean upon

Some are very antsy
And just cannot sit still
Some just can't be quiet
They never have and never will

Some are teacher's pets
They crave your all attention
One or two never say a word
Some even fear suspension

Most are just kids being kids
Some are quite exceptional
Others have special needs
One needs a meeting in the hall

Some kids pick their nose
One kid can't tie his shoes
One kid needs go to the bathroom
One is getting abused

One child has a crush on you
One kid collects bugs
One no one can stand
But they all just need a hug

And no matter how you feel
On any given day
You show up and do what's expected
For not nearly enough pay

Staying up at night grading papers
And creating lesson plans
Spending your own money to buy supplies
That no one understands

Parent/Teachers conferences
Don't forget the PTA
Cafeteria duty and field trips
All in just one day

I know this because I've been there
And stood on all sides of your desk
Student, parent, volunteer, and teacher
But I can tell that you are the best

You are the first responders
And this I know is for real
Because if it were not for you
All other positions in life could not be filled

Thank you for your dedication
Educators one and all
Thanks for standing up in front of us
With your backs against the wall
So, hats off to all the teachers!!!

"The Traveler"

July 19th, 2023

As I travel across this land
From sea to shining sea
I begin to learn just who I am
And what kind of man I must be

In this land of milk and honey
Where we have so much to give
It's hard to find the money
That we need to live

Even in this wonderful place
There is darkness at every turn
Where children live in such disgrace
No living can they earn

Why must we be so stoic
Towards those who can only cry
Yet we act so heroic
As we go passing by

What have I done today
To help my fellow man
Go on his merry way
If I do not lend a hand

So, reach for my hand my brother
And I will lift you up
For there may not be another
To gladly fill your cup

What would Jesus do?
If He were here instead
Why! He would gladly give his coat
And His last morsel of bread

I can do no less
If it's a Christian that I am
So I will gladly bless
Another fellow man

And I will count my blessings
As I travel on my way
And be thankful for the things I have
And be careful of what I say

For others may not know
The one who died for them
So it's my job to let it show
Joyfully from within

For when my time here is over
And I look back and find
That no matter how life was
No one I left behind

I can go home knowing
That I did my very best
His Love through me was showing
And I passed the test

When I enter Heaven's Gates
And His Face I see
Then I'll sing Halleluiah
Forever Triumphantly!!!

The Winds of Change

August 27th, 2023

The winds of change blew over me
Like waves along the shore
The darkness engulfed me entirely
And, the light in me shined no more

A million tears I cried
I was In such great despair
No hope was to be found
Alone without a prayer

I was floating on a sea of tears
With no rescue in sight
As the storm continued to rage
On that long and lonesome night

Finally with the morn
And the rising of the sun
I could see the land
A new day had just begun

As I reached the sandy beach
I stopped and looked left and right
And made a chance decision
That would forever change my life

Because of that decision
I found you
Another lost soul searching
And you found me too...

"Think of Me"
August 8th, 2023

When you are feeling blue
And maybe a wee bit lonely
Close your eyes and breathe
Then just think of me

I am there somewhere
Inside your head I'll be
In your heart and soul
Alive in your memories...

"Thinking of You"
August 15th, 2023

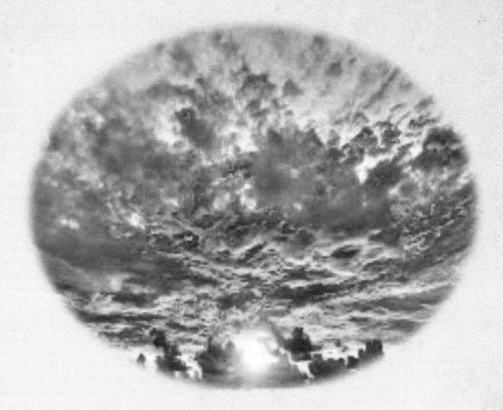

I slumber naught thinking of you
Tossing and turning all thru the night
And when I rise up in the morning
You are the sunshine of my life...

"Till the Journey's End"

August 24th, 2023

When I first set out into this world
I was lost and all alone
And I was so very blessed
When you finally came along

Then we started off together
Arm in arm and hand in hand
Knowing we could pass all tests
As we traveled across this land

Then came the day while I was gone
That you met your fate
Now once again I'm all alone
For I've lost my mate

Inside the garden wall
By the rocky ledge
I sat beside your grave
And I began to plead and beg

Asking God just "Why"
He had to take you so far away
What am I supposed to do
I can't carry on this way

The pain is overwhelming
My heart may never mend
But, I know that you are in my soul
Till the journey's end...

"Today I Crossed the Burning Bridge"

July 30th, 2023

Today I found myself
Crossing the burning bridge
When I could no longer handle
Walking up on the ridge

For one of my darkest fears
Became greater than the other
When I chose an evil enemy
Over a friend that's been my brother

What a fool I've been
To treat someone this way
Now I have to take this burden
All the way to my grave

Forgiveness is not possible
For someone who has passed
The sin I've committed against them
Will for eternity last

This is the most unforgivable crime
In the history of creation
So, I am doomed now to spend
An eternity in abomination

Hell could not be as hot
As the torment that I am in
How I chose a known evil enemy
And sacrificed my own friend

I know it isn't possible
But Lord hear my plea
Because I am truly sorry
For this foolish discrepancy

After all that we have been through
And all we have endured together
How could I just toss away a love
I thought should have lasted forever

So, my oldest and dearest friend
I weep violently on your grave
For I know that I should not have
Sacrificed you in this way

My pain is so great
I cannot carry on at all
So I ask you for forgiveness
Before I on my own sword fall

I know I am not worthy
So, I must surely die
Just to keep myself
From living with this lie

I only wish things could be different
And that I had died honorably in war
Fighting the greatest mortal enemy
We have ever known before

Hear me now my brother
For I have surely failed
My God, family, and countrymen
The ship bearing my forgiveness has sailed

Today I Crossed The Burning Bridge...

"Today I Woke Up Smiling"

August 4th, 2023

Today I woke up smiling
At the thought of you
How you make me laugh
The way you used to do

It is such a comfort
In my mind your voice I hear
Feeling you in my heart
Knowing that you are near

Always and forever
You are my very soul
And I have your memory
To consider when I am old

It's going to be an awesome day
All because of you
You're the light unto my path
And I'll never more be blue

So, thank you for everything you've said
And for all that you have taught me
That helps me be the person
That I ought to be

My goals for today are these:
1. Be positive in what I say and do
2. Spread the Word of God
3. And have a grateful attitude!!!

"Today"

August 4th, 2023

Today is the first day
Of the rest of my life
It's up to me to make it the best
Despite the pain and the strife

Today I get to try again
The things I failed before
To climb back up the ladder
And up from off the floor

Today I get the opportunity
To lend a helping hand
And create a way up and out
For someone else if I can

Today I am the reason
That someone else can smile
I put myself in their shoes
And walk that extra mile

Today is the day
That I reach someone for Christ
And show them that He is the way
The truth and the light...

"Together"

August 16th, 2023

Together we were as
Two halves of a heart
Who had searched
Both near and far

To find each other
Here in this place
And become raptured
In loves embrace

We persisted to weather
Life's many storms
And faced all our demons
They took many forms

We lived, laughed, and loved
And then we cried
Thru many troubles and trials
But we survived

Then came the day
You were ripped from my grasp
My countenance grew dim
So, I donned a mask

An imaginary smile
For others to see
But, I was dying inside
It hurt so painfully

Depression and heartbreak
Soon settled in
And it didn't take much
To get under my skin

I built many walls
To hide behind
Keeping others away
But, soon I would find

Your love and memories
Became so very strong
Convincing me that I
Was living all wrong

So, I reached for your spirit
And you took my hand
Pulling back from
The sinking quicksand

I was drowning in pain
I was drowning in sorrow
But, your love's brought me here
To the edge of tomorrow

Now, I feel as if
I can carry on
Accepting the fact
That you're really gone

But, I am not here
So all alone
Your memory still lingers
In my heart like a song

"True Love Endures"

August 26th, 2023

When the world around you crumbles
Remember that true love endures
When the night seems to last forever
Of this you can be sure

When the pain of loss consumes you
And you're down to your last tear
Remember that true love endures
When your loved ones are nowhere near

So, when you are down and out
Get down upon your knees
Ask the Lord for guidance
For understanding and for peace

And remember when you pray
Those faithful pleas of yours
That God alone can testify
That true love endures...

"Under the Crescent Moon"

August 16th, 2023

I still remember the night we met
When you made my poor heart swoon
That's when I fell in love
Under the crescent moon

We were too tired to do the Tango
So, we waltzed all night long
We didn't stop to catch our breath
Until the night was gone

And you held my hand so tightly
As I walked you to your room
That's when we fell in love
Under the crescent moon

Now you may think I'm crazy
For writing you this way
But my love keeps getting stronger
And I can't wait another day

So, now I'm down on one knee
And this I'm going to do
Will you accept my proposal
Out here under the crescent moon

Now it's been a long, long time
Since we waltzed the whole night thru
Long ago and far away
From the place that we once knew

So, blame it all on the time we spent
Out there under the crescent moon...

"Victory in Jesus"

August 16th, 2023

I was a lonesome loser for so long
Till Christ I came to know
He saved me from my sins
And from the fires down below

He died on the tree
A cross for him was made
He gladly did his father's will
And the price for my sins was paid

He died there on that cross
Oh! What a price he paid
He conquered Hell and death
When he arose from the grave

Many songs have been written
About that eventful day
And his ultimate sacrifice
So, all our sins could be washed away

So, go on, get up and shout and
You will understand why he saved us
His is the King of Kings
And we have Victory in Jesus!!!

"Walk a Mile in His Shoes"

By Brian W. Woodward
22 March 2017
Walk a mile in his shoes
A cliché we have heard a lot
But how many have actually done this?
Many? I think not
For the veteran returning home
From a war, he could not win
Only to keep on fighting
Again, again, and again
He has no one to hold him
On those long and scary nights
When every noise reminds him
Of the battle and the fights
The wounds that he carries
Both inside and out
Wreak havoc on his very soul
As life tosses him about
Sometimes he can't help himself
Or the things that he does
And he constantly pushes away
The ones that he loves
So when you say your prayers tonight
Don't forget the lonely Vets
That fought the fight in your place
Just so that you might rest

Veterans
Thank you for your service
And the pain that you endure
For the freedom which isn't free
of this we know for sure
For you all are in our prayers
And in our every thought
We lift you up to our Lord
From our heart of hearts

"When I Die"

August 5th, 2023

Do not be sad when I die
Do not be blue when I pass
I will be in a better place
In Heaven with Him at last

Many happy trails will I travel
On Golden Streets will I walk
Many friends will I see again
And to my Savior talk

You should all envy me
It's a wonderful journey I will take
With a brand new body
Without all the pains and the ache's

Do not a funeral for me have
But a Celebration of my life
For I've been given life eternal
With Christ Jesus on High

Now do not shed useless tears
Or long for me weep
But go and do something good
From someone who is in need

For death is but a portal
Through time and space
That takes you another world
To a better time and place...

"Your Love Still Lingers"

August 17th, 2023

Even though you are gone
Over to the shores of Heaven
And I have been going through
This very great depression

Your love still lingers on
It's in everything you touched
No matter where I am in here
I can feel it oh, so much

It's what gets me through each day
And keeps me holding on so tight
So that I can make it through
The long and lonely nights

Thank you for that gift
It keeps giving again and again
The spirit of your love is here
I feel it every time I breathe in

Thank you for watching over me
As I stumble through my day
I feel as if you are oh so near
Even though you are far away

I love you and I miss you
And I long to hear your voice
You left so very quickly
But I know you had no choice

You know I will be okay
Eventually
Thank you for the way
That you still care for me

When you drift back up to Glory
Say hello to the Lord for me
Because when my time here o'er
It's with you again I'll be...

"Your Love"

September 1st, 2023

Your love really moves me
To be a better man
To be better at the things I do
And better than what I am

Your love has a passion
That cannot be replaced
It has an inner beauty
More than just your pretty face

You're everything I dream of
When I have time to dream
Your love keeps me going
When I run out of steam

Your love keeps me coming back
All part of your magnetic charm
Your love will keep me alive
And safe from all harm

And on that final day
And in our finest hour
Your love will see me through
It has that kind of power

Rivaled only by the gods
Who sit way up on high
Your love has the strength
To carry me till I die

Do not ever for one second doubt
That you are my heart and soul
For your love is what I live for
And it will be till I am gray and old

And in the life hereafter
We'll walk hand in hand
Through the gates of Heaven
Together in Glory Land...

"Your Smile"

September 3rd, 2023

It's the first thing I long to see
When I wake in the morning light
And the thing that puts me to sleep
When I lay down at night

Your smile brings me happiness
It never makes me cry
Your smile brings me comfort
When I don't know the reasons why

Your smile lifts me up
When I'm down and out
Your smile shows me the answers
When my mind is filled with doubt

Your smile is the sunshine
That brightens up my day
Your smile makes me laugh
When my troubles get in the way

Your smile brightens up a room
When you enter there
Your smile cancels out the negative
With your positive stare

I could go on and on forever
About your lovely smile
But there's not enough ink and paper
And the words would stretch for miles...

Milton Keynes UK
Ingram Content Group UK Ltd.
UKHW050233100124
435724UK00003B/58